Essential
Programming

AI Foundations

Essential Programming

AI Foundations

Sergio Ramírez Gallardo

Index

## Chapter 1

Introduction to AI and Its Impact

Definition of Artificial Intelligence

Artificial Intelligence (AI) is a branch of computer science that focuses on creating systems capable of performing tasks that, when carried out by humans, require intelligence. These tasks include learning, problem-solving, perception, natural language understanding, and decision-making.

Analogy: The Human Brain and AI

To better understand what AI is, we can compare it to the human brain. Just as our brain processes information, learns from past experiences, and makes decisions based on that information, AI systems also process data, learn from it, and can make decisions or predictions. However, unlike the human brain, AI operates through algorithms and mathematical models programmed by humans.

Types of AI

AI can be classified into different categories based on its level of sophistication and capabilities. Below are the main types of AI with more detailed explanations:

- **Weak or Narrow AI**: Designed to perform a specific task, such as voice recognition, product recommendations, or language translation. These systems do not possess consciousness or general understanding and operate under a limited set of constraints and objectives defined by their programmers. A common example of weak AI is virtual assistants like Siri or Alexa, which can answer questions and execute specific commands but do not deeply understand context or possess knowledge beyond their programmed functions.

- **General AI**: Aims to imitate human cognitive ability across a wide variety of tasks. A general AI can understand, learn, and apply knowledge in different domains similarly to how a human does. This type of AI is still theoretical and does not exist in current practice. Creating a general AI would involve overcoming numerous challenges, including understanding context, creativity, and the ability to transfer knowledge across different areas.

- **Superintelligent AI**: Refers to an AI that surpasses human intelligence in all aspects, including creativity, decision-making, and social skills. This concept is futuristic and is subject to intense debates within the scientific and philosophical community regarding its ethical and security implications. Superintelligent AI could potentially solve complex problems that are currently beyond human capability, but it also poses significant risks if not properly managed.

- **Skills/Expertise-based AI**: Within weak AI, there are

subcategories based on specific skills. These include:

- **Natural Language Processing (NLP)**: Enables machines to understand and generate human language.

- **Computer Vision**: Equips machines to interpret and process images and videos.

- **Robotics**: Involves the creation of physical machines that can perform tasks in the real world.

- **Recommendation Systems**: Use algorithms to suggest products, services, or content to users based on their preferences and previous behaviors.

- **Hybrid AI**: Combines different AI approaches and techniques to leverage the strengths of each. For instance, a hybrid AI might integrate deep neural networks with symbolic methods to enhance both perception and logical reasoning.

Additional Classification Based on Functionality

Another way to classify AI is by its functionality and capacity to interact with the environment:

- **Reactive AI**: Lacks memory and learning capacity; responds to current stimuli without considering past experiences. An example would be Deep Blue, the chess computer that defeated Garry Kasparov in 1997.

- **Limited Memory AI**: Can utilize past experiences to make future decisions. Many current AI systems, such as autonomous vehicles, fall into this category as they use historical data to improve their predictions and actions.

- **Theory of Mind AI**: A theoretical category where AI has the capability to understand the emotions, beliefs, and thoughts of other agents, allowing for more human and empathetic interactions.

- **Self-aware AI**: Still hypothetical, this AI would possess self-awareness and a subjective understanding of itself and its environment, similar to human consciousness.

History and Evolution of AI

The history of Artificial Intelligence is marked by cycles of enthusiasm and skepticism, significant advancements, and periods of stagnation known as "AI winters." Below is a timeline of the most relevant milestones in the evolution of AI:

Origins and Early Concepts

- **Antiquity**: The idea of intelligent machines has existed in mythologies and legends since ancient times. For example, Greek mythology talks about automatons created by gods.

- **18th and 19th Century**: With the advancement of mathematics and logic, the foundations were laid for the development of machines that could perform calculations and logical tasks.

The Era of Computing and Early Algorithms

- **1943**: Warren McCulloch and Walter Pitts present a mathematical model of an artificial neuron, laying the groundwork for neural networks.

- **1950**: Alan Turing publishes the influential paper "Computing Machinery and Intelligence," where he poses the question "Can machines think?" and proposes the famous Turing Test as a criterion for intelligence.

- **1956**: The Dartmouth conference is held, considered the official birth of AI as an academic discipline. Researchers focus on the idea that all human intelligence can be described in a way that a machine can simulate it.

The First Decades: Optimism and Early Systems

- **1950s and 1960s**: Development of the first AI programs, such as Alan Turing's chess program and ELIZA, a natural language processing program that simulated a conversation.

- **1970s**: Emergence of expert systems, like MYCIN, designed to diagnose infectious diseases. These systems use logical rules to make decisions in specific domains.

Pragmatism and AI "Winters"

- **1980s**: Increased investment in AI and development of more complex models. However, a lack of complete understanding and insufficient hardware led to a decrease in interest and funding, known as the first "AI winter."

- **1990s**: Resurgence of interest due to advances in machine learning and the availability of large datasets. More efficient algorithms are developed, and computing power is improved.

The Modern Era: Big Data, Deep Learning, and Large Language Models

- **2000s and beyond**: Explosion of digital data and hardware improvements enable the development of deep learning models, which have revolutionized fields such as computer vision and natural language processing.

- **2010s**: Emergence of large language models like **GPT (Generative Pre-trained Transformer)** from OpenAI. These models, including **ChatGPT**, are based on transformer architectures that allow for coherent and contextually relevant text generation, facilitating advanced applications in chatbots, machine translation, and content generation.

- **Present Day**: AI has become an integral part of numerous everyday applications, from virtual assistants to recommendation systems and autonomous vehicles. In addition, there is a trend towards **explainable** and **ethical AI**, focusing on the transparency and fairness of algorithms to mitigate biases and ensure responsible use of technology.

Current Applications of AI in Different Industries

Artificial Intelligence has permeated a wide variety of industries, transforming processes, improving efficiency, and opening new possibilities. Below are some of the most notable applications in different sectors:

Healthcare

- **Medical Diagnosis**: AI systems can analyze medical images, such as X-rays and MRIs, to identify anomalies with high precision.

- **Personalized Medicine**: Algorithms analyze genomic data to design specific treatments for each patient.

- **Data Management**: AI optimizes the management of medical records, facilitating quick access to and analysis of information.

Finance

- **Fraud Detection**: Machine learning algorithms monitor transactions in real-time to identify suspicious patterns.

- **Algorithmic Trading**: Automated systems execute stock trades based on data analysis and predictive models.

- **Financial Advisory**: Robo-advisors provide personalized investment recommendations based on user profiles.

Transportation

- **Autonomous Vehicles**: Self-driving cars use AI to navigate, detect obstacles, and make real-time decisions.

- **Route Optimization**: Algorithms plan efficient routes to reduce travel time and fuel consumption.

- **Traffic Management**: Intelligent systems monitor and manage traffic flow to minimize congestion.

Retail and E-commerce

- **Recommendation Systems**: Platforms like Amazon and Netflix use AI to suggest personalized products and content to users.

- **Inventory Management**: AI optimizes inventory control by anticipating demand and reducing waste.

- **Customer Service**: Chatbots and virtual assistants enhance customer experience by providing quick and accurate responses.

Manufacturing

- **Predictive Maintenance**: Algorithms analyze sensor data to predict machinery failures and schedule preventive maintenance.

- **Process Automation**: Intelligent robots perform repetitive tasks with high precision and efficiency.

- **Quality Control**: Computer vision systems inspect products in real-time to ensure quality standards.

Agriculture

- **Precision Agriculture**: AI analyzes sensor and satellite data to optimize irrigation, fertilization, and harvesting.

- **Crop Monitoring**: Drones equipped with AI inspect the health of crops, identifying pests and diseases.

- **Automation of Agricultural Tasks**: Agricultural robots perform tasks like planting and harvesting, improving efficiency and reducing costs.

Entertainment and Media

- **Content Creation**: Algorithms generate music, art, and texts, enabling new forms of artistic expression.

- **Experience Personalization**: Streaming platforms adjust recommendations and user experiences based on preferences and behavior.

- **Sentiment Analysis**: AI analyzes comments and opinions on social media to assess the reception of products and content.

Education

- **Personalized Tutoring**: AI systems adapt educational content to meet the needs and learning paces of each student.

- **Automated Assessment**: Algorithms grade exams and assignments, providing immediate feedback.

- **Performance Analysis**: AI identifies areas for improvement and helps educators design more effective strategies.

Practical Example: AI in the Healthcare Industry

Case Study: Breast Cancer Diagnosis with AI

A hospital implemented an AI system to analyze mammograms with the goal of improving early detection of breast cancer. The system uses convolutional neural networks (CNNs) to identify patterns in images that may indicate tumor presence. After training the model with thousands of labeled images, the system achieved accuracy comparable to that of experienced radiologists, significantly reducing diagnosis time and allowing for earlier interventions.

Benefits of AI in Industries

- **Efficiency and Automation**: The ability to perform repetitive tasks and process large volumes of data quickly and accurately.

- **Informed Decision Making**: Advanced data analysis provides valuable insights for strategic decision-making.

- **Personalization**: Tailoring products and services to the individual needs and preferences of users.

- **Error Reduction**: Greater accuracy in critical tasks, such as medical diagnoses or quality inspection.

Challenges and Considerations

Despite the numerous benefits, implementing AI also presents challenges:

- **Ethics and Privacy**: Responsible use of data, avoiding privacy violations and making ethical decisions.

- **Bias in Models**: Ensuring that algorithms do not perpetuate existing biases in training data.

- **Transparency and Explainability**: Making AI systems understandable and transparent for users and developers.

- **Technological Dependence**: Avoiding excessive reliance on technology while maintaining human control over critical decisions.

Conclusion

Artificial Intelligence has come a long way from its theoretical beginnings to becoming an omnipresent technology that transforms multiple industries. Its ability to process and analyze large volumes of data, learn from it, and make informed decisions opens up a multitude of unprecedented possibilities. However, alongside its benefits, AI poses ethical and technical challenges that must be addressed with responsibility and rigor.

This chapter has provided an overview of what AI is, its historical evolution, and its current applications across various industries. In the upcoming chapters, we will delve into the foundations of programming with Python, data structures, and the essential algorithms that form the backbone of AI systems.

## Chapter 2

Philosophy and Ethics of Artificial Intelligence

Introduction

Artificial Intelligence (AI) not only represents a significant technological advancement but also raises profound philosophical and ethical questions. As AI systems become increasingly integrated into everyday life, it is crucial to understand the ethical implications that accompany their development and use. This chapter explores the philosophical and ethical considerations that arise in the context of AI, analyzing its social and labor impact as well as the responsibility and biases inherent in AI systems.

Ethical Considerations in AI Development

Definition of Ethics in AI

Ethics in AI refers to the set of principles and norms that guide the development, implementation, and use of artificial intelligence systems. These principles aim to ensure that AI benefits society, minimizes harm, and respects individual rights and freedoms.

Fundamental Ethical Principles

1. **Beneficence and Non-Maleficence**: AI systems should be designed to benefit humanity and avoid causing harm. This involves ensuring that AI does not perpetuate abuses or is used for harmful purposes.

2. **Autonomy**: Respecting individuals' capacity to make informed decisions. AI should support, not replace, human agency.

3. **Justice**: Ensuring that the benefits and burdens of AI are distributed fairly, avoiding discrimination and promoting inclusivity.

4. **Transparency**: The processes and decisions of AI should be understandable and accessible to users and developers.

5. **Accountability**: Establishing clear mechanisms for accountability for actions and decisions made by AI systems.

Common Ethical Dilemmas

- **Privacy**: The extensive use of personal data by AI systems can invade individual privacy.

- **Informed Consent**: Individuals should know how their data is used and give explicit consent.

- **Power Inequality**: The concentration of advanced technology in a few hands can exacerbate social and economic inequalities.

Practical Examples

- **Facial Recognition**: Used to enhance security but raises concerns about mass surveillance and privacy.

- **Recommendation Systems**: Personalize user experience but may create filter bubbles that limit exposure to diverse information.

Social and Labor Impact of AI

Transformation of the Labor Market

AI-driven automation is redefining the labor landscape. While it creates new opportunities, it can also eliminate certain types of jobs.

Example: Automation in Manufacturing

Robots and automated systems have replaced many repetitive tasks in factories, increasing efficiency but reducing the need for human labor in those specific roles.

New Job Opportunities

AI also generates jobs in emerging areas such as:

- **Algorithm Development**: Professionals specialized in designing and improving AI models.

- **AI Ethics and Regulation**: Experts working on creating policies and standards for the ethical use of AI.

- **AI System Maintenance and Oversight**: Personnel responsible for ensuring the correct and safe functioning of AI systems.

Social Challenges

- **Economic Inequality**: The gap between those with skills to work with AI and those without may widen, exacerbating social inequalities.

- **Job Displacement**: Jobs that depend on repetitive tasks are especially susceptible to automation, which may lead to increased unemployment if labor transitions are not managed adequately.

Practical Example: AI in the Healthcare Sector

Automated Medical Diagnosis

AI can analyze medical images with high precision, supporting doctors in diagnosis. Although it improves efficiency and accuracy, it also requires reskilling of healthcare professionals to work alongside new technologies.

Accountability and Bias in AI Systems

Accountability in AI

Determining who is responsible when an AI system makes an error or causes harm is a complex challenge. Possible areas of accountability include:

- **Developers and Companies**: Responsible for designing and testing AI systems.

- **End Users**: Those who implement and operate AI systems in their specific environments.

- **Government Regulators**: Charged with establishing and enforcing regulations governing AI use.

Types of Bias in AI

AI systems can perpetuate and amplify biases present in the data they are trained on. Some common types of bias include:

- **Data Bias**: Incomplete or non-representative data leading to unjust decisions.

- **Algorithmic Bias**: Biased decisions arising from how models are designed and trained.

- **User Bias**: Biased interpretations of the results generated by AI.

Mitigating Bias

1. **Data Diversification**: Ensuring that datasets used to train AI are varied and representative of different demographic groups.

2. **Algorithm Audits**: Regularly reviewing algorithms to identify and rectify potential biases.

3. **Transparency in Design**: Documenting and making public the processes of design and training of models for evaluation and oversight purposes.

Examples of Bias in AI

- **Facial Recognition**: Studies have shown that some facial recognition systems have higher error rates when identifying individuals from minority ethnic groups due to non-representative training datasets.

- **Credit Application Processing**: Algorithms that reject credit applications from certain demographic groups based on historical data patterns reflecting previous discrimination.

Philosophy of AI

Nature of Intelligence

The philosophy of AI addresses fundamental questions about the nature of intelligence and consciousness. Some key questions include:

- **Can machines think?**: Exploration of whether an AI can possess a form of awareness or understanding similar to that of humans.

- **Theory of Mind**: Considering whether AI can develop empathy, emotions, or intentional mental states.

The Problem of Consciousness in AI

One of the deepest philosophical debates is whether an AI can be genuinely conscious or if it merely simulates conscious behavior.

Analogy: The Ecosystem Analogy

Imagine a simulation of an ecosystem on a computer. Although the system may replicate complex interactions between organisms, the question arises whether the digital organisms truly experience life or are merely following programmed guidelines. Similarly, while an AI can simulate intelligent behavior, it is unclear whether it possesses true consciousness.

Autonomy and Free Will

The possibility of AI acting autonomously raises questions about concepts like free will and independent decision-making.

- **Determinism vs. Free Will**: Can machines have freedom of action, or are they limited by their predefined algorithms?

- **Autonomous Agents**: AI systems that operate without direct human intervention pose questions about their capacity to make ethical decisions.

Legal Framework and Regulation of AI

Need for Regulation

The rapid advancement of AI has led to a growing demand for legal frameworks overseeing its development and use, ensuring adherence to ethical standards and protection of individual rights.

Global Initiatives

Various international bodies are working on guidelines and regulations for AI. For example:

- **European Union**: Has proposed strict regulations addressing aspects such as transparency, accountability, and safety of AI systems.

- **United Nations (UN)**: Promotes ethical principles for AI development through its specialized agencies.

Challenges of Regulation

- **Pace of Innovation**: Regulations often struggle to keep up with rapid technological development, leading to legal gaps.

- **Globalization**: AI is a global technology, making it difficult to implement consistent regulations on an international scale.

- **Balancing Regulation and Innovation**: It is crucial to find a balance that protects society without stifling technological innovation.

Ethics in the Design and Development of AI Systems

Human-Centered Development

Prioritizing human needs and values in the design of AI systems to ensure they serve to enhance people's lives. This involves engaging end users in the development process, understanding their expectations and concerns, and designing solutions that truly address relevant problems. A human-centered approach also considers usability, accessibility, and the emotional impact of AI technologies, ensuring that these tools are inclusive and beneficial for all segments of society.

Inclusion and Diversity in Development Teams

Encouraging diversity in AI development teams to minimize biases and ensure that different perspectives are considered. Diverse teams, including individuals from different genders, ethnicities, cultures, and disciplines, can identify and mitigate biases that might otherwise go unnoticed. Additionally, the variety of experiences and knowledge within the team enriches the creative and technical process, allowing the development of more robust and equitable solutions. Inclusion is not just an ethical issue; it also enhances the quality and relevance of developed AI systems.

Ethical Impact Assessment

Implementing ethical impact assessments throughout the AI development cycle to identify and address potential issues before implementation. These assessments should consider aspects such as privacy, security, fairness, and social well-being. By conducting proactive analyses, developers can anticipate and mitigate potential risks, ensuring that AI systems operate responsibly. Ethical impact assessments also promote transparency and accountability, establishing a foundation for trust between users and society at large.

Transparency and Explainability

Designing AI systems that are transparent and whose decision-making processes are understandable to users and stakeholders. Transparency involves providing clear information on how algorithms function, what data they utilize, and how decisions are made. Explainability goes a step further, allowing users to understand the reasons behind specific AI decisions. This not only fosters trust and acceptance of technology but also facilitates the identification and correction of errors or biases within systems. Transparency and explainability are essential for ensuring that AI acts ethically and in alignment with human values.

Future of Ethics in AI

Explainable AI (XAI)

Explainable AI (XAI) aims to create systems whose processes and decisions are comprehensible even to those without deep technical knowledge. As AI becomes more complex and ubiquitous, the need for clear and accessible explanations becomes essential to foster trust and public acceptance. XAI addresses this challenge by developing methods and tools that allow users to interpret and understand how and why AI reaches specific conclusions. This not only facilitates monitoring and error diagnosis but also empowers users to make informed decisions regarding the use of technology.

Multidisciplinary Collaboration

Integrating perspectives from various disciplines—such as philosophy, sociology, and law—into AI development to address its ethical complexities. Multidisciplinary collaboration enriches the approach to ethics in AI, allowing for a more holistic understanding of the social, cultural, and legal impacts of emerging technologies. Philosophers may contribute ethical frameworks and value analyses, sociologists may provide insights into social dynamics and inequalities, and legal experts can ensure compliance with regulations and the protection of individual rights. This integration of diverse knowledge is fundamental to developing AI systems that are genuinely beneficial and fair for society.

Education and Awareness

Promoting education and awareness concerning the ethical implications of AI among both developers and the general public. Ethical training should be an integral part of AI education, ensuring that professionals understand and value the importance of ethical considerations in their daily work. Moreover, it is crucial to educate the public about how AI works, its benefits, and risks, to foster informed and participatory dialogue about the future of technology. Training programs, university courses, and public awareness campaigns are effective tools for increasing understanding and ethical responsibility in the use of AI.

Legal Framework and Regulation of AI

Need for Regulation

The rapid advancement of AI has led to a growing demand for legal frameworks overseeing its development and use, ensuring adherence to ethical standards and protection of individual rights.

Global Initiatives

Various international bodies are working on guidelines and regulations for AI. For example:

- **European Union**: Has proposed strict regulations addressing aspects such as transparency, accountability, and safety of AI systems.

- **United Nations (UN)**: Promotes ethical principles for AI development through its specialized agencies.

Challenges of Regulation

- **Pace of Innovation**: Regulations often struggle to keep up with rapid technological development, leading to legal gaps.

- **Globalization**: AI is a global technology, making it difficult to implement consistent regulations on an international scale.

- **Balancing Regulation and Innovation**: It is crucial to find a balance that protects society without stifling technological innovation.

Practical Activities

1. **Case Analysis**: Investigate a recent case where an AI system displayed significant biases. Analyze the causes, consequences, and measures taken to mitigate the issue.

2. **Ethical Debate**: Divide participants into two groups. One group defends the broad use of AI in facial recognition to improve public safety, while the other group argues against it due to privacy and bias concerns.

3. **Development of a Personal Ethical Code**: Create a document outlining your own ethical guidelines for the development and use of AI systems, considering aspects such as transparency, privacy, and fairness.

4. **Simulation of Ethical Impact Assessment**: Use a hypothetical AI development case (e.g., a customer service chatbot) and conduct an ethical impact assessment, identifying potential risks and proposing solutions.

Reflection Questions

1. **Should legal responsibility be granted to the creators of AI systems that make errors? Why or why not?**

2. **How can companies balance innovation in AI with ethical concerns relating to user privacy?**

3. **What measures can be implemented to minimize biases in facial recognition systems?**

4. **Is it possible to achieve true general AI, and if so, what ethical implications would it have?**

5. **How can society ensure that the benefits of AI are distributed equitably and not just to economic elites?**

Summary

This chapter has explored the complex intersections between artificial intelligence, philosophy, and ethics. From defining fundamental ethical principles to analyzing challenges and future trends in regulation and design of AI systems, the importance of a conscious and multidisciplinary approach has been emphasized to ensure that technology advances fairly and responsibly. Practical activities and reflection questions encourage readers to deepen their understanding and ethical commitment, paving the way for a future where AI contributes positively to society.

## Chapter 3

Overview of Artificial Intelligence

Introduction

Artificial Intelligence (AI) has evolved exponentially over the past few decades, becoming an integral part of many industries and the daily lives of individuals. This chapter will provide an overview of the subfields that make up AI, current trends and future directions, as well as notable case studies that illustrate the applicability and potential of artificial intelligence across various areas.

Subfields of AI

AI is a broad and multifaceted field encompassing various areas of study and application. Below are the main subfields of AI:

Machine Learning

Machine learning is a branch of AI focused on creating algorithms and models that allow machines to learn from data. Through different techniques, systems can make predictions or decisions based on patterns in the data. There are two main approaches:

- **Supervised Learning**: The machine is trained with a dataset that includes known inputs and outputs. For example, a model may be trained to predict house prices based on features such as size, location, and number of rooms, where it is provided with examples of previous sales.

- **Unsupervised Learning**: The machine is confronted with unlabeled data and must identify patterns or groupings on its own. An example would be clustering customers in a business to identify similar groups for marketing campaigns.

Natural Language Processing (NLP)

Natural language processing is the subfield focused on the interaction between computers and human language. This includes tasks such as machine translation, sentiment analysis, and text generation. Tools like chatbots and virtual assistants use NLP to understand and respond to user inquiries. An example is the Google Cloud Natural Language API, which allows developers to analyze text content to extract relevant information.

Computer Vision

Computer vision enables machines to interpret and understand images and videos from the visual world. This field has gained momentum thanks to convolutional neural networks (CNNs), which are particularly effective in classification and object identification tasks. Common applications include:

- **Facial Recognition**: Used by platforms like Facebook to tag users in photographs.

- **Object Detection**: Used in autonomous vehicles to identify obstacles and pedestrians.

Robotics

Robotics combines AI with engineering to design and build machines that can perform physical tasks. Robots can be programmed to carry out repetitive jobs in factories, perform complex surgeries in medicine, or keep public spaces clean through automatic vacuums. Increasingly, robots are equipped with machine learning capabilities to adapt to changing environments.

Expert Systems

Expert systems are computer programs that simulate the decision-making ability of a human expert in a specific domain. Using a set of rules and specialized knowledge, these systems can offer recommendations or diagnoses. For example, **MYCIN** was one of the first expert systems, designed to diagnose infectious diseases.

Reinforcement Learning

Reinforcement learning is a subfield where an agent learns to make decisions by interacting with its environment, receiving rewards or penalties based on its actions. This approach is used in areas like video games and process automation. A notable example is AlphaGo, the program that defeated the world champion in Go by learning to play this complex game without prior exposure to the rules.

Trends and Future Directions of AI

Increased Explainability and Transparency

With the growth of AI in critical applications, such as healthcare and justice, there is an urgent call for AI systems to be more explainable and transparent. This means models must be able to provide understandable reasons for their decisions so that humans can trust them. New methodologies are being developed to create explainable AI (XAI), allowing developers and users to understand the processes behind AI decisions.

Ethical and Responsible AI

As AI continues to expand, there is a heightened focus on developing technologies that are not only efficient but also ethical and responsible. Organizations and governments are establishing guidelines and legal frameworks to ensure the ethical development of AI, considering social impacts, biases, and data privacy. The implementation of ethical principles in the design of AI systems is a trend that will continue to grow.

AI and Big Data

AI and Big Data are intrinsically linked, as the efficiency of AI algorithms depends on the quantity and quality of available data. The ability to process and analyze large volumes of data in real-time will continue to develop, enabling companies to customize services, anticipate trends, and generate more accurate insights.

Integration of AI in All Sectors

From healthcare to agriculture, AI will increasingly be integrated into industries, enhancing efficiency, productivity, and the quality of products and services. Precision agriculture, where data is used to optimize resource use, is an area that promises significant growth.

Augmented AI

The combination of humans and machines to achieve optimized results (augmented AI) is another exciting future direction. Instead of completely replacing humans, augmented AI seeks to enhance human capabilities in the workplace, leading to closer collaboration between people and machines.

Notable Case Studies

Case Study 1: Automated Medical Diagnosis

A hospital implemented a machine learning-based AI system to analyze X-ray images. By training the model with thousands of labeled images, doctors were able to improve accuracy in detecting diseases such as pneumonia. This approach not only increased early detection rates but also optimized the time radiologists needed to spend on each image.

Case Study 2: Autonomous Vehicles

Technology companies like Waymo have developed autonomous vehicles that use computer vision and AI to navigate complex environments.

Equipped with multiple sensors and algorithms that interpret data in real-time, these vehicles can drive safely, detect obstacles, and make decisions in dynamic situations, such as pedestrians crossing the street.

Case Study 3: Virtual Assistants

Google Assistant and Amazon Alexa are examples of virtual assistants that use natural language processing to interact with users. These systems can respond to inquiries, perform tasks like scheduling reminders, and control smart home devices. As they advance, their ability to understand context and dialogue is becoming increasingly sophisticated.

Conclusions

AI is redefining the way we live and work, with applications spanning from healthcare to transportation and beyond. With a solid understanding of its subfields and current trends, we will be better equipped to anticipate and face the future of artificial intelligence. This overview prepares us for the upcoming chapters, where we will delve into the tools and techniques necessary to develop effective and ethical AI projects. As we continue to explore the vast world of AI, it is essential to maintain a critical and proactive mindset regarding its opportunities and challenges.

## Chapter 4

Python Installation

Introduction

Python, a versatile programming language, has become one of the fundamental pillars in the field of artificial intelligence and data science. Its clear syntax, rich libraries, and vast supportive community make Python an excellent choice for both beginners and experts. In this chapter, we will explore the process of installing and configuring Python, ensuring that our development environment is ready to start programming AI solutions.

Downloading and Installing Python

Choosing the Version

Python has two main versions: Python 2.x and Python 3.x. **Python 3** is the recommended version, as it is the one that continues to receive support and updates. Most modern Python libraries have dropped support for Python 2, so make sure to download Python 3.

Downloading the Installer

1. Visit the official Python page: https://www.python.org/downloads/.

2. Click on the download button corresponding to your operating system (Windows, macOS, or Linux).

3. When downloading the installer, save the file in a location that is easy to remember.

Installation on Windows

1. **Run the Installer**: Double-click on the file you downloaded.

2. **Installer Options**:

   ◦ Make sure to check the option: "Add Python to PATH". This will facilitate running Python from the command line.

3. **Select Installation**: You can choose between "Install Now" for a standard installation or "Customize installation" to select additional features. The standard installation is suitable for most users.

4. Once the installation is complete, close the installer.

Installation on macOS

1. **Run the Installer**: Double-click on the .pkg file you downloaded.

2. **Follow the Instructions**: Accept the terms and conditions and follow the steps to complete the installation.

3. When finished, open the terminal and verify the installation using the command:

```
1  python3 --version
```

Installation on Linux

In most Linux distributions, Python is already installed. However, if you need to install or update it, you can use your distribution's package manager.

For **Ubuntu** or **Debian**, run the following command in the terminal:

```
1  sudo apt update
2  sudo apt install python3
```

For **Fedora**, you can use:

```
1  sudo dnf install python3
```

After the installation, verify it with:

```
1  python3 --version
```

Setting Environment Variables

In a standard Python installation on Windows, the option to add Python to the PATH variable is usually set automatically. However, if you need to configure it manually, follow these steps:

Configuration on Windows

1. Right-click on "This PC" or "My Computer" on the desktop and select "Properties".

2. Click on "Advanced system settings".

3. In the system properties window, click on "Environment Variables".

4. Under "System Variables", look for the variable named `Path` and select "Edit".

5. Click "New" and enter the path where Python is installed, usually `C:\Python39\` for Python 3.9 (adjust the number according to the installed version) and `C:\Python39\Scripts\`.

6. Save the changes and close the windows.

Configuration on macOS and Linux

Generally, the installation of Python on macOS and Linux automatically configures the necessary environment variables. However, if you need to add a shortcut to Python, you can modify your user profile file (e.g., `.bashrc` or `.bash_profile`).

Open the terminal and add the following line at the end of the file:

```
1   export PATH="$PATH:/usr/local/bin/python3"
```

Then, apply the changes by running:

```
1   source ~/.bashrc  # Or ~/.bash_profile as applicable
```

Verifying the Installation

Once Python is installed, it is crucial to verify that everything is working properly.

Verifying Python

Open a terminal (or command line on Windows) and type:

```
1  python3 --version
```

Or on Windows, try:

```
1  python --version
```

You should see the version of Python you just installed. If you see an error message, review the steps you performed earlier.

Verifying pip

pip is the package manager for Python and is used to install additional libraries and packages. To check if **pip** is installed, run:

```
1  pip3 --version
```

Or on Windows:

```
1  pip --version
```

If necessary, you can install **pip** using the following command:

```
1   python3 -m ensurepip
```

Setting Up Virtual Environments

In software development, especially in the field of artificial intelligence and data science, it is essential to maintain a controlled and organized working environment. This is where **virtual environments** come in.

What Are Virtual Environments?

Virtual environments are isolated programming environments that allow you to have their own dependencies and installed packages, separate from the global Python environment on your system. By creating a virtual environment, you can install different versions of the libraries needed for your project without interfering with other projects or applications that may require different versions of the same libraries.

Why Are Virtual Environments Useful?

1. **Dependency Isolation**: You avoid conflicts between different projects that require different versions of the same libraries. For example, if one project requires numpy version 1.18 and another requires version 1.19, virtual environments allow both to function without issues.

2. **Simplified Management**: They facilitate the installation and management of specific libraries for a project, making it clean and easy to perform necessary updates and changes.

3. **Testing**: They allow you to experiment with new libraries or versions without risking disruption to the stable environments of other projects.

How to Work with Virtual Environments

Creating a Virtual Environment

1. Open a terminal and navigate to the directory where you want to create your project.

2. Create a new virtual environment by running:

```
1   python3 -m venv my_env
```

This will create a folder named `my_env` in your current directory.

Activating the Virtual Environment

- **On Windows**:

```
1   my_env\Scripts\activate
```

- **On macOS and Linux**:

```
1   source my_env/bin/activate
```

Once activated, you will see the name of the virtual environment at the beginning of your command line, indicating that all operations performed with `pip` or `python` are taking place within this environment.

Installing Packages Inside the Virtual Environment

With the virtual environment activated, you can install packages without affecting the global Python environment. Use **pip** to install packages such as `numpy`, `pandas`, and `matplotlib`:

```
1  pip install numpy pandas matplotlib
```

This ensures that these libraries are only available in your virtual environment and do not interfere with other configurations you may have.

To deactivate the virtual environment, simply run:

```
1  deactivate
```

This will return you to the global environment of your system.

Conclusion

In this chapter, we have covered all the necessary steps to download, install, and configure Python, as well as how to work with virtual environments. This foundation is essential for delving into artificial intelligence development and data manipulation. In the following chapters, we will begin to explore the fundamental concepts of Python and how to use them in the context of artificial intelligence.

## Chapter 5

Integrated Development Environments (IDEs) for Python

Introduction

An integrated development environment (IDE) is an application that combines various tools and features designed to help programmers develop software more efficiently. In the context of Python and artificial intelligence, having a good IDE can make a significant difference in developer productivity, optimizing code writing, debugging, and management. In this chapter, we will explore several popular IDEs for Python, their features, and basic setup and customization so that you can navigate your development environment effectively.

What is an IDE?

An IDE is not just a simple text editor; it is a robust set of tools that have been integrated to provide a cohesive and optimized programming environment. When dealing with software development, programmers face various complex tasks that require the use of multiple tools. An IDE addresses this need by grouping these tools in one place, providing a smoother and less fragmented working experience. Among the most defining features of an IDE is the code editor, which not only allows for code writing but also includes features like syntax highlighting, improving readability and allowing programmers to identify errors more quickly.

In addition to the editor, an IDE typically includes a debugger that allows developers to identify and efficiently correct errors in their code. Instead of having to review the code line by line, the debugger allows setting breakpoints and following the execution flow, which facilitates the detection of logical or syntactical errors.

The compiler or interpreter is another cornerstone of any IDE, as these components allow executing the code that one has written. While Python is an interpreted language, most IDEs offer options that help in managing code execution, allowing quick result viewing and facilitating the trial-and-error cycle.

Project management is another valuable feature provided by an IDE. Good organization of files and folders within a project is essential for maintaining clarity and efficiency, especially in larger projects. An IDE allows managing this structure intuitively, making it easy to create new files and efficiently organize resources.

Lastly, many modern IDEs include version control support, which is essential in the world of collaborative development. Tools like Git can be integrated, allowing developers to track changes in their code over time. This not only helps avoid losing work but also facilitates collaboration between teams by maintaining rigorous control over what changes have been made and by whom.

In summary, an IDE is vital not only for efficiency in code writing but also to minimize errors, manage projects effectively, and foster a collaborative environment, all of which is crucial especially in the dynamic field of artificial intelligence.

Popular IDEs for Python

PyCharm

PyCharm is one of the most popular and comprehensive IDEs for Python development. Developed by JetBrains, it offers many integrated tools that can help you become more efficient and productive. Among its standout features is code autocompletion, which automatically suggests variable names, classes, and methods as you type, speeding up your workflow. It also has a powerful code refactoring feature that makes modifying existing code safely easier, improving its readability and structure. The integrated debugger allows setting breakpoints and following program execution step-by-step, which is fundamental for identifying errors.

Installing PyCharm

1. Visit the official PyCharm website.

2. Select the version you prefer: **Community** (free) or **Professional** (with more features).

3. Click the download button corresponding to your operating system (Windows, macOS, or Linux).

4. Once the download is complete, open the installer.

5. On Windows, select "Next" to accept the terms and conditions.

Make sure to check the "Add Python to PATH" option for easier execution.

6. Follow the instructions in the installation wizard and click "Install."

7. Once the installation is complete, open PyCharm.

8. Set up your initial project by selecting "Create New Project" and configuring the preferences (including the Python interpreter to be used).

9. Customize the IDE according to your preferences, such as the theme and keyboard shortcuts.

Visual Studio Code

Visual Studio Code (VS Code) is a lightweight yet very powerful code editor developed by Microsoft. Although it is considered more of an editor than a "full" IDE, its flexibility allows it to be effectively configured to function as a development environment for Python. VS Code features a minimalist interface that emphasizes focusing on the code, and it also includes an integrated terminal that makes it easy to run command lines directly from the editor.

Installing Visual Studio Code

1. Go to the official Visual Studio Code website.

2. Click the download button corresponding to your operating system.

3. Once the installer is downloaded, start the installation process.

4. Accept the terms and conditions and select "Next" until you reach the "Install" option.

5. Once installed, open Visual Studio Code.

6. Upon opening it for the first time, go to the extensions tab (square icon on the left sidebar).

7. Search for "Python" and install the official Python extension.

8. Configure the options according to your preferences, such as the theme and font.

Jupyter Notebook

Jupyter Notebook is a widely used tool in academic and scientific settings, especially for data analysis. It allows the creation of interactive documents that combine code, text, and visualizations. One of the most notable features of Jupyter is its ability to mix annotations with functional code, allowing the use of Markdown to document your work while executing code in real time. This is extremely useful not only for development but also for presenting results and conclusions.

Installing Jupyter Notebook

1. Ensure you have Python and `pip` installed on your system.

2. Open a terminal or command line.

3. Run the following command to install Jupyter Notebook:

```
pip install notebook
```

4. Once the installation is complete, run the following command to start Jupyter Notebook:

```
jupyter notebook
```

5. This will open a new window or tab in your browser where you can create new notebooks and start working on your analysis.

Anaconda

Anaconda is more than just an IDE; it is a complete distribution geared towards data science that includes Jupyter and many other necessary libraries for effective work in this field. Its most well-known IDE is **Spyder**, which resembles MATLAB and is specifically designed to facilitate data analysis and visualization. Anaconda simplifies the creation and management of work environments, which is essential in data science projects that may require different libraries and configurations.

Installing Anaconda

1. Visit the official Anaconda website.

2. Download the installer corresponding to your operating system (Windows, macOS, or Linux).

3. Open the downloaded installer.

4. Accept the license terms and select "Next."

5. Choose between an installation for "Just Me" or "All Users" and click "Next."

6. Select the directory where you want to install Anaconda and click "Next."

7. Make sure the option "Add Anaconda to my PATH Environment variable" is checked if you want to use Anaconda from the terminal.

8. Click "Install" and wait for the installation to complete.

9. Once completed, you can open **Anaconda Navigator** from your

start menu.

10. From Anaconda Navigator, you can start **Spyder** and have access to all the tools needed to work on your artificial intelligence and data science projects.

IDE Comparison

Here's a comparison table summarizing some of the main features of the described IDEs:

Feature	PyCharm	VS Code	Jupyter Notebook	Anaconda (Spyder)
Code Editor	Yes	Yes	Yes	Yes
Integrated Terminal	Yes	Yes	No	Yes
Debugger	Yes	With extension	No	Yes
Git Integration	Yes	Yes	No	Yes
Plugin Support	Yes	Extensive (extensions)	No	No
Ideal for AI	Very suitable	Very suitable	Ideal for analysis	Very suitable

Usage Recommendations

Choosing the right IDE will depend on your specific needs. If you are a beginner, **VS Code** or **Jupyter Notebook** would be good options due to their ease of use and flexibility. For more serious software development projects, **PyCharm** stands out due to its powerful refactoring and debugging features. Take time to customize your development environment, as adjusting the color scheme, shortcuts, and other preferences can make your programming experience more enjoyable and efficient.

Additionally, consider integrating version control tools, such as **Git**, into your workflow. The previously mentioned IDEs offer functionalities for this, smoothing the management of your projects and collaborations.

Conclusion

In this chapter, we explored the importance of integrated development environments for Python and how they can positively impact your programming process. By choosing the IDE that best suits your needs along with a personalized setup, you can maximize your productivity in developing artificial intelligence solutions. As you continue advancing in your learning, becoming familiar with different IDEs and their features will be key to your success in the world of programming with Python. In the next chapter, we will begin delving into the fundamentals of Python from scratch, preparing you to develop your AI projects.

Managing Virtual Environments and Dependencies

Introduction

In software development, especially in projects that involve multiple libraries and dependencies, proper management of the development environment becomes crucial. Oftentimes, projects may require different versions of the same libraries or even have dependencies that could conflict with one project or another. Fortunately, Python offers tools that allow creating virtual environments to help keep each of these projects isolated. In this chapter, we will discuss what virtual environments are, why they are important, how to create and manage one using `venv` and `conda`, and how to install and manage dependencies using `pip`.

What are Virtual Environments?

A **virtual environment** is a self-contained environment that allows a project to have its own dependencies and installed packages without interfering with other projects that may be running on the same system. Imagine that every time you start a project, a "box" is built where you can store all the libraries and settings necessary for that project, without mixing with "boxes" of other projects. This is especially useful when working on multiple projects that require different configurations and library versions.

Importance of Virtual Environments

Using virtual environments provides several benefits:

1. **Dependency Isolation**: Each project has its specific set of dependencies, avoiding conflicts. For example, you can have one project that requires `numpy` version 1.18 and another that needs version 1.20; with virtual environments, both can coexist without issues.

2. **Simplified Management**: They make it easier to install and uninstall specific libraries for a project, allowing for easier management of the necessary versions.

3. **Reproducible Environments**: When collaborating, you can use a file that specifies all the dependencies needed for a project, making it easy for other developers to replicate the same environment.

4. **Safe Execution**: Virtual environments allow you to experiment with new libraries or versions without damaging the global environment or affecting other projects.

Creating and Managing Virtual Environments with ,[object Object]

Creating a Virtual Environment

The `venv` module is a built-in tool in Python that allows for easy creation of virtual environments. Below, we will explain how to do this.

1. Open the terminal or command line.

2. Navigate to the directory where you want to create your virtual environment. For example, if you want to create a virtual environment called `my_env`, type:

```
1  mkdir my_projects
2  cd my_projects
```

3. To create the virtual environment, run the following command:

```
1  python3 -m venv my_env
```

This will create a folder named `my_env` in your current directory, which will contain an installation of Python and a space to install packages.

Activating the Virtual Environment

To use the created virtual environment, you need to activate it. This changes the context of Python and `pip` to the new environment.

- **On Windows**:

```
1   my_env\Scripts\activate
```

- **On macOS and Linux**:

```
1   source my_env/bin/activate
```

Once activated, you will see the name of the virtual environment appearing at the beginning of the command line, indicating that all future operations will be performed within this environment.

Installing Dependencies

Once the virtual environment is active, you can install any necessary library using `pip`. For example, if you want to install `numpy`, simply type:

```
1   pip install numpy
```

This will install `numpy` only in the virtual environment, without affecting other Python installations on your system.

Deactivating the Virtual Environment

After you have finished your work, it is good practice to deactivate the virtual environment to return to the global Python environment. To do this, simply type:

```
1   deactivate
```

This will close the virtual environment, and the prompt will revert to its previous state.

Creating and Managing Virtual Environments with ,[object Object]

The **Anaconda** environment manager offers another option for creating and managing virtual environments. Below, I will show you how to do this.

Installing Anaconda

If you do not have **Anaconda** installed yet, you can download it from its official site and follow the instructions for your operating system.

Creating a Virtual Environment with conda

To create a new virtual environment using conda, open a terminal and run the following command:

```
1  conda create --name my_env python=3.9
```

Here, my_env is the name you are giving to your new environment, and you can specify the version of Python you want.

Activating the Virtual Environment

To activate the virtual environment you just created, type:

```
1  conda activate my_env
```

You will see the name of the environment appear in your terminal, confirming that you are now working within it.

Installing Dependencies

Similar to `pip`, you can install packages using `conda`. For example, to install `numpy`, you would run:

```
1  conda install numpy
```

This will download and install `numpy` and its dependencies, ensuring that all are compatible.

Deactivating the Virtual Environment

To deactivate the environment, simply type:

```
1  conda deactivate
```

This will take you back to the global environment.

Installing and Managing Dependencies with ,[object Object]

`pip` is the official package manager for Python and is used to install and manage libraries. You can use it within a virtual environment (recommended) or in a global environment.

Installing Packages

To install a package, simply run:

```
1  pip install package_name
```

For example:

```
1  pip install pandas
```

Listing Installed Packages

To see a list of all libraries installed in your current environment, use:

```
1  pip list
```

Updating a Package

If you want to update a library to the latest version, use:

```
1  pip install --upgrade package_name
```

Uninstalling a Package

To uninstall a package you no longer need, run:

```
1  pip uninstall package_name
```

Creating a Requirements File (`requirements.txt`)

A common practice is to create a file called `requirements.txt` that contains all the dependencies of your project with their specific versions. This allows others to easily reproduce the environment. To create this file, run:

```
1  pip freeze > requirements.txt
```

To install dependencies from this file, use:

```
1  pip install -r requirements.txt
```

Conclusion

In this chapter, we have explored the importance of virtual environments in the development of Python projects. With tools like `venv` and `conda`, it is possible to effectively manage dependencies and avoid conflicts between projects. By implementing them properly, you can ensure that each of your projects has the appropriate environment to function smoothly. In the next chapter, we will examine the basic syntax of Python, where we will begin our journey into the world of programming with this powerful language.

Basic Syntax of Python

Introduction

The syntax of a programming language is the set of rules that defines how code should be written. In Python, the syntax is clear and concise, making it easier to learn and use even for those who are just starting in the world of programming. In this chapter, we will explore the basic syntax of Python, covering fundamental elements that are the foundation for effective development in this language. From the structure of a program to the use of comments and script execution, this chapter will provide a solid foundation for continuing your learning.

Structure of a Python Program

A program in Python is a series of instructions that are executed sequentially, from the first line to the last. Each line of code represents an action that the Python interpreter will carry out. This is akin to a set of instructions given to a person to complete a task, where each step must be followed in order to achieve the final result.

What is interesting about Python is that it does not require the use of symbols like semicolons at the end of each line, unlike many other programming languages. This helps the code look cleaner and easier to read, allowing you to focus more on what you are trying to achieve rather than the exact syntax used.

Starting with "Hello, World!"

A traditional way to start programming in any language is to create a program that simply prints "Hello, world!" to the screen. This example is not only a programming classic, but also illustrates how to interact with the system through code:

```
1  print("Hello, world!")
```

Here we break down this code:

- `print()` is a built-in function in Python that is used to display text on the screen.
- What is inside the parentheses, `"Hello, world!"`, is a string that will be passed to the function for it to print.

To execute this code, you need to save it in a file with a `.py` extension, for example, `hello_world.py`. Then, you can use the terminal command line to run it:

```
1  python hello_world.py
```

When you do this, you should see "Hello, world!" printed in the console.

Common Elements in a Python Program

1. **Line of Code**: Each instruction you give to the program is written on a line. In Python, if you want the code to execute correctly, it must be properly indented using spaces or a tab. This is essential, as Python uses indentation to define blocks of code.

2. **Functions**: Functions are blocks of code that perform specific tasks. In our previous example, `print()` is a function. You can create your own functions that execute when you call them, thereby organizing your code into manageable parts.

3. **Comments**: Comments are parts of the code that do not execute but are used to add explanations or annotations. They are valuable when working in a team or when the code may be reviewed in the future.

Here's an example that includes all these concepts:

```
1   # This script prints a greeting to the user.
2   name = input("What is your name? ")
        # Asks for the user's name
3   print(f"Hello, {name}!")
        # Prints the greeting using the variable
```

In this example, the line beginning with # is a comment. The second line prompts the user to enter their name and stores it in the variable `name`. Finally, the last line prints a greeting that includes the user's name.

Comments and Formats

Comments are lines of code that do not execute and are used to document or explain parts of the code. In Python, comments can be made in two ways:

1. **Single-line Comments**: Use the # symbol.

```
1  # This is a single-line comment
2  print("Hello, world!")
        # Prints a message to the console
```

2. **Multi-line Comments**: Using triple single ' ' ' or triple double quotes " " ".

```
1  """
2  This is a multi-line comment
3  """
4  print("Hello, world!")
```

Comments are very useful for clarifying the intent of the code and facilitating teamwork, as other programmers can quickly understand what has been done.

Executing Scripts

Executing scripts in Python is made easy by its interpretive nature. There is no need to compile the code beforehand; you can simply run the .py file with the Python command in the terminal, as shown earlier. This allows for rapid iteration and testing.

For example, you could save the following code in a file called example.py:

```
1  # My first script in Python
2  name = "John"
3  print(f"Hello, {name}!")
```

After saving the file, you can run the script in the terminal, and you should see the result in the console:

```
1  python example.py
```

Conclusion

Knowing and understanding the basic syntax of Python is fundamental for any programmer aiming to master this language. Through simple examples and clear explanations, we have explored how a program in Python is structured, the importance of indentation, how to use comments to document code, and how to execute scripts. This foundation will allow you to confidently progress to more complex topics and make the most of the capabilities that Python has to offer in the world of artificial intelligence and beyond.

Data Types and Operators

Introduction

In any programming language, data types are fundamental as they define how data can be manipulated and managed within a program. Python, being a dynamically typed language, allows data types to be determined automatically at runtime, making both programming and data handling easier. In this chapter, we will explore the different data types available in Python and the operators we can use to work with them. This way, we will better understand how to manipulate data in our programs and make the most of the functionalities that Python offers.

Data Types in Python

Python has several built-in data types, which we can classify into various categories. Below, we will analyze each of these types in detail.

Numeric Data Types

Numeric data types in Python are essential for performing calculations and mathematical operations. They are primarily divided into two categories:

- **Integers (`int`)**: These are whole numbers without a decimal part. They can be positive, negative, or zero.

```
1   age = 30
2   height = -175
```

- **Floating-point numbers (`float`)**: These are numbers that contain a decimal part.

```
1   temperature = 36.6
2   pi = 3.14159
```

- **Complex numbers (`complex`)**: These have a real part and an imaginary part. Their format is `a + bj`, where `a` and `b` are real numbers and `j` represents the imaginary unit.

```
1   complex_number = 2 + 3j
```

Common Functions

Python provides various functions for working with numbers. Some of the most relevant are:

- `abs(x)`: Returns the absolute value of `x`.

```
1  result = abs(-5)  # result is 5
```

- `round(x, n)`: Rounds the number x to n decimal places.

```
1  rounded = round(3.14159, 2)  # rounded is 3.14
```

- `max(*args)` and `min(*args)`: Return the maximum and minimum of a series of numbers.

```
1  maximum = max(1, 3, 7, 2)  # maximum is 7
2  minimum = min(1, 3, 7, 2)  # minimum is 1
```

- Mathematical functions from the `math` module:

  - `math.sqrt(x)`: Returns the square root of x.

```
1  import math
2  square_root = math.sqrt(16)
   # square_root is 4.0
```

  - `math.sin(x)`, `math.cos(x)`: Return the sine and cosine of x (in radians).

  - `math.pow(x, y)`: Returns x raised to the power of y.

```
1  power = math.pow(2, 3)  # power is 8.0
```

Text Data Types

In Python, the text data type is represented by strings. They are defined using single (' ') or double (" ") quotes. Strings are immutable, meaning they cannot be modified once created.

```
1  first_name = "John"
2  last_name = 'Doe'
```

We can also perform operations with strings, such as concatenation, which joins two or more strings.

```
1  full_name = first_name + " " + last_name
2  print(full_name)  # Output: John Doe
```

Common Functions

Some common functions for working with strings in Python include:

- `len(s)`: Returns the length of the string `s`.

```
1  length = len(first_name)  # length is 4
```

- `strip()`: Removes whitespace from the beginning and end of the string.

```
1  clean_string = "   Hello   ".strip()
      # clean_string is "Hello"
```

- `lower()` and `upper()`: Converts the string to lowercase or uppercase.

```
1  lowercase = first_name.lower()
```

```
    # lowercase is "john"
2   uppercase = last_name.upper()  # uppercase is "DOE"
```

- `replace(old, new)`: Replaces all occurrences of `old` with `new` in the string.

```
1   new_string = "Hello John".replace("John", "Peter")
    # new_string is "Hello Peter"
```

- `find(sub)`: Returns the position of the first occurrence of `sub`, or -1 if not found.

```
1   position = first_name.find("o")  # position is 1
```

Sequential Data Types

Sequential data types allow the storage of collections of elements. The most common are:

- **Lists (`list`)**: Ordered and mutable collections that can contain elements of different types.

```
1   fruits = ["apple", "banana", "cherry"]
```

- **Tuples (`tuple`)**: Ordered and immutable collections, which means they cannot be changed after creation.

```
1   coordinates = (10.0, 20.0)
```

- **Strings (`str`)**: As we mentioned earlier, they are a type of sequence that stores text.

Common Functions

For lists:

- `append(x)`: Adds the element x to the end of the list.

```
1   fruits.append("orange")
        # fruits is ["apple", "banana", "cherry",
        "orange"]
```

- `remove(x)`: Removes the first occurrence of the element x.

```
1   fruits.remove("banana")
        # fruits is ["apple", "cherry", "orange"]
```

- `sort()`: Sorts the elements of the list in place.

```
1   fruits.sort()
        # fruits is ["cherry", "apple", "orange"]
```

- `index(x)`: Returns the index of the first occurrence of the element x.

```
1   index = fruits.index("apple")   # index is 1
```

For tuples, since they are immutable, they cannot be modified. However, you can use:

- `count(x)`: Counts how many times the element x appears in the tuple.

```
1  repeated = (1, 2, 3, 1, 1).count(1)  # repeated is 3
```

Set Data Types

Sets (set) are collections of unordered and unique elements, meaning there cannot be duplicate elements. They are used to perform mathematical operations such as union and intersection.

```
1  fruits = {"apple", "banana", "cherry"}
```

Common Functions

Common operations with sets include:

- add(x): Adds an element x to the set.

```
1  fruits.add("kiwi")  # fruits now includes "kiwi"
```

- discard(x): Removes an element x from the set if it exists.

```
1  fruits.discard("banana")
      # "banana" is removed without error, even if it
      doesn't exist
```

- union(y): Returns a new set that is the union of two sets.

```
1  other_fruits = {"pear", "kiwi"}
2  union_fruits = fruits.union(other_fruits)
     # union_fruits is {"apple", "cherry", "kiwi",
     "pear"}
```

- `intersection(y)`: Returns a new set that contains only the elements that are in both sets.

```
1  set1 = {1, 2, 3}
2  set2 = {2, 3, 4}
3  intersection = set1.intersection(set2)
     # intersection is {2, 3}
```

Map Data Types

Maps in Python are represented by dictionaries (`dict`). They are collections of key-value pairs where each key must be unique. Dictionaries are mutable and allow access to values through their keys.

```
1  person = {
2      "name": "John",
3      "age": 30,
4      "height": 1.75
5  }
```

Common Functions

Some common functions for working with dictionaries are:

- `get(key)`: Returns the value associated with the key, or a default value if the key does not exist.

```
1   age = person.get("age")   # age is 30
```

- `keys()`: Returns a view of all the keys in the dictionary.

```
1   keys = person.keys()
    # keys is a view of ["name", "age", "height"]
```

- `values()`: Returns a view of all the values in the dictionary.

```
1   values = person.values()
    # values is a view of ["John", 30, 1.75]
```

- `items()`: Returns a view of the key-value pairs as tuples.

```
1   items = person.items()
    # items is a view of [("name", "John"), ("age",
    30), ("height", 1.75)]
```

- `update(other)`: Updates the dictionary with the key-value pairs from another dictionary.

```
1   person.update({"weight": 70})
    # person now includes weight
```

Operators in Python

Operators are symbols that allow us to perform operations on data types. Python includes several types of operators, and below we focus on arithmetic, comparison, and logical operators.

Arithmetic Operators

These operators allow performing basic mathematical calculations.

- **Addition (+)**: Adds two operands.

```
1  a = 5
2  b = 10
3  sum = a + b  # sum is 15
```

- **Subtraction (-)**: Subtracts the second operand from the first.

```
1  subtraction = b - a  # subtraction is 5
```

- **Multiplication (*)**: Multiplies two operands.

```
1  multiplication = a * b  # multiplication is 50
```

- **Division (/)**: Divides the first operand by the second, as long as the second is not zero.

```
1  division = b / a  # division is 2.0
```

- **Floor Division (//)**: Returns the integer part of the division.

```
1  floor_division = b // a  # floor_division is 2
```

- **Modulus (%)**: Returns the remainder of the division.

```
1  remainder = b % a  # remainder is 0
```

- **Exponentiation (**)**: Raises the first operand to the power of the second.

```
1  power = a ** 2  # power is 25
```

Comparison Operators

Comparison operators allow comparing values and return a boolean result (True or False).

- **Equal to (==)**: Checks if two values are equal.

```
1  is_equal = (a == b)  # is_equal is False
```

- **Not equal to (!=)**: Checks if two values are different.

```
1  is_different = (a != b)  # is_different is True
```

- **Greater than (>) and Less than (<)**: Compare values to see which is greater or lesser.

```
1  greater = (b > a)  # greater is True
2  lesser = (a < b)  # lesser is True
```

- **Greater than or equal to (>=) and Less than or equal to (<=)**: Check if a value is greater than or equal to, or less than or equal to another.

```
1  greater_equal = (b >= a)  # greater_equal is True
2  lesser_equal = (a <= b)  # lesser_equal is True
```

Logical Operators

Logical operators are used to combine boolean expressions.

- **AND (and)**: Returns `True` if both expressions are true.

```
1  result = (a < b) and (b > 0)  # result is True
```

- **OR (or)**: Returns `True` if at least one of the expressions is true.

```
1  result = (a > b) or (b > 0)  # result is True
```

- **NOT (not)**: Inverts the logical value of the expression.

```
1  result = not (a < b)  # result is False
```

Conclusion

Understanding data types and operators in Python is essential for developing effective and efficient programs. Throughout this chapter, we have explored the various data types that Python offers and how to use them effectively through the available operators. This foundation will allow you to continue developing more advanced programming skills and apply this knowledge to real-world problems in artificial intelligence and other fields. In the next chapter, we will address control flow structures, which will enable our code to make decisions and execute different pathways based on the conditions we define.

Control Flow Structures

Introduction

Control flow structures are fundamental in any programming language. They allow a program to make decisions, repeat actions, and alternate between different execution paths based on certain conditions. In Python, we have various structures that facilitate the creation of complex logic in our programs. This chapter examines the three most common control flow structures in Python: conditional statements (`if`, `elif`, `else`), loops (`for` and `while`), as well as loop control using the `break`, `continue`, and `pass` statements.

Conditional Statements

Conditional statements allow a program to execute different blocks of code based on whether certain conditions are met. In Python, we use the `if` statement for this.

The `if` Statement

The basic structure of an `if` statement looks like this:

```
1   if condition:
2       # Code to execute if the condition is true
```

The `condition` can be any expression that evaluates to `True` or `False`. If it is `True`, the indented block of code under `if` is executed. If it is `False`, the program's flow moves beyond the block.

Example

Let's imagine we want to check if a person can vote based on their age:

```
1   age = 18
2
3   if age >= 18:
4       print("You are eligible to vote.")
```

In this case, if `age` is 18 or more, it will print "You are eligible to vote."

The `else` Statement

The `else` statement is used to define a block of code that will run if the condition of the `if` is `False`:

```
1   if condition:
2       # Code if the condition is true
```

```
3  else:
4      # Code if the condition is false
```

Example

Continuing with the previous example, we can add an `else`:

```
1  age = 16
2
3  if age >= 18:
4      print("You are eligible to vote.")
5  else:
6      print("You are not eligible to vote.")
```

Here, if the age is less than 18, it will print "You are not eligible to vote."

The `elif` Statement

Sometimes, it is necessary to check multiple conditions. For this, we use `elif`, which is short for "else if":

```
1  if condition1:
2      # Code if condition1 is true
3  elif condition2:
4      # Code if condition2 is true
5  else:
6      # Code if none of the conditions are met
```

Example

Suppose we want to classify age into groups:

```
1  age = 25
2
3  if age < 12:
4      print("You are a child.")
5  elif age < 18:
6      print("You are a teenager.")
7  else:
8      print("You are an adult.")
```

In this case, the program will print "You are an adult." because the age is 25.

Loops

Loops allow you to repeat a block of code multiple times. In Python, there are two main types of loops: for and while.

The for Loop

The for loop allows you to iterate over a sequence (like a list, tuple, or string). Its basic syntax is:

```
1  for variable in sequence:
2      # Code to execute on each iteration
```

Example

Let's say we want to print the elements of a list of fruits:

```
1   fruits = ["apple", "banana", "cherry"]
2
3   for fruit in fruits:
4       print(fruit)
```

This code will print each of the fruits in the list.

The while Loop

The while loop executes a block of code as long as a condition is true:

```
1   while condition:
2       # Code to execute while the condition is true
```

Example

Let's imagine we want to count to 5:

```
1   counter = 1
2
3   while counter <= 5:
4       print(counter)
5       counter += 1  # Increments the counter by 1
```

This loop will print numbers from 1 to 5.

Controlling Flow within Loops

Sometimes, it is necessary to control the flow within loops using the `break`, `continue`, and `pass` statements.

The `break` Statement

The `break` statement is used to exit a loop before it completes its normal cycle. This can be useful if a specific condition is met.

Example

Suppose we want to count to 5, but we want to stop if we reach 3:

```
1  counter = 1
2
3  while True:  # Infinite loop
4      if counter == 3:
5          break  # Exits the loop when counter is 3
6      print(counter)
7      counter += 1
```

This code will print 1 and 2, and then it will exit the loop.

The `continue` Statement

The `continue` statement skips to the next iteration of the loop, omitting the code that follows in the same iteration.

Example

Let's say we want to print numbers from 1 to 5 but skip the number 3:

```
1  for number in range(1, 6):
2      if number == 3:
3          continue
   # Skips the rest of the code for this number
4      print(number)
```

This code will print 1, 2, 4, and 5.

The pass Statement

The pass statement is used as a placeholder. It is useful when a statement is syntactically required but no action is needed.

Example

```
1  for number in range(1, 6):
2      if number == 3:
3          pass  # Does nothing, just continues
4      else:
5          print(number)
```

This code will work the same way as the previous one, printing 1, 2, 4, and 5, but the pass statement occupies the place in the loop where another logic could go.

Conclusion

In this chapter, we have explored control flow structures in Python, including conditional statements and loops. These tools are essential for enabling our programs to make decisions and repeat operations logically and efficiently. By mastering the use of `if`, `elif`, `else`, `for`, `while`, along with the control statements `break`, `continue`, and `pass`, you will be well-prepared to handle more complex logic in your programming projects and artificial intelligence applications. In the next chapter, we will continue exploring fundamental concepts in Python, specifically about functions and modules.

## Chapter 10

Functions and Modules in Python

Introduction

Functions and modules are two fundamental concepts in Python and programming in general. They allow us to break down code into smaller, more manageable parts, promoting code reuse and organization. Functions encapsulate a sequence of instructions that perform a specific task, while modules allow us to group related functions into a single file. This chapter explores how to define and use functions, how to create modules, the importance of both in the development of artificial intelligence programs and software in general, and the concept of recursion.

Functions in Python

A function in Python is a block of code designed to perform a specific task. Functions can take inputs (known as parameters) and return outputs (results), making them powerful tools for simplifying and organizing code.

Defining Functions

To define a function in Python, we use the `def` keyword, followed by the function name and parentheses that may contain parameters. Here is a basic example:

```
1  def greet(name):
2      print(f"Hello, {name}!")
```

In this example, we have defined a function called `greet` that takes one parameter: `name`. When this function is called, it prints a personalized greeting.

Calling a Function

To use a function, we simply call it by its name and pass the necessary arguments:

```
1  greet("John")  # Output: Hello, John!
```

Parameters and Arguments

Functions can accept different types of parameters, whether positional, keyword, or default values.

Positional Parameters

Positional parameters are those that must be passed in the order they are defined in the function.

```python
1  def add(a, b):
2      return a + b
3
4  result = add(5, 3)  # result is 8
```

Keyword Parameters

Keyword parameters allow us to specify the value of the parameters when calling them, regardless of their position.

```python
1  def introduce(name, age):
2      print(f"I am {name} and I am {age} years old.")
3
4  introduce(age=30, name="Ana")
     # Output: I am Ana and I am 30 years old.
```

Parameters with Default Values

We can also define parameters that have default values. If no argument is provided for these parameters, the default value will be used.

```python
1  def greet(name="guest"):
2      print(f"Hello, {name}!")
3
4  greet()  # Output: Hello, guest!
```

Returning Values

Functions can return values using the `return` keyword. The returned value can be stored in a variable for later use.

```python
1  def multiply(a, b):
2      return a * b
3
4  result = multiply(4, 5)  # result is 20
```

Nested Functions

Python also allows us to define functions within other functions. This can be useful to encapsulate logic that is only relevant within a specific function.

```python
1  def operation(a, b):
2      def add(x, y):
3          return x + y
4
```

```
5        return add(a, b)
6
7    result = operation(2, 3)  # result is 5
```

Recursion

Recursion is a powerful concept where a function calls itself to solve problems. This approach is useful for breaking down complex problems into simpler subproblems. Each recursive call must have a base case that stops the recursion to prevent infinite loops.

Example of a Recursive Function

A classic case to illustrate recursion is the calculation of the factorial of a number. The factorial of a number n (denoted as n!) is the product of all positive integers from 1 to n. For example, 5! is 5 x 4 x 3 x 2 x 1 = 120.

We can define a recursive function to calculate the factorial as follows:

```
1  def factorial(n):
2      if n == 0:  # Base case
3          return 1
4      else:
5          return n * factorial(n - 1)  # Recursive call
6
7  result = factorial(5)  # result is 120
```

In this example, the `factorial` function calls itself with a decreasing value of n until n equals 0, where it returns 1, thus ending the recursion.

Best Practices with Functions and Modules

Applying best practices when creating functions and modules not only improves code readability but also facilitates collaboration with other developers and long-term maintenance. Here are some best practices along with their importance and practical examples:

1. **Descriptive Names**: Use clear and descriptive names for functions and modules. This helps others (and yourself in the future) quickly understand what the code does.

```
1  def calculate_rectangle_area(base, height):
   # Descriptive
2      return base * height
```

2. **Documentation**: Document your functions using docstrings to explain their purpose and the parameters they accept. This is helpful for understanding a function's functionality without reading its implementation.

```
1  def add(a, b):
2      """Returns the sum of two numbers."""
3      return a + b
```

3. **Modularity**: Divide your code into modules that group related functions. This makes it easier to organize and manage the code. For example, you might have a module for mathematical operations and another for input/output operations.

```
1  # math_operations.py
2  def add(a, b):
3      return a + b
```

4. **Reusability**: Design functions that can be reused in different contexts to reduce code duplication. This not only saves time but also minimizes errors.

```python
1  def print_message(message):
2      print(message)
3
4  print_message("Hello")
       # Can be reused in different parts of the code
```

5. **Avoid Side Effects**: Aim for your functions not to modify external variables. This makes the behavior of functions predictable, making them easier to understand and use.

```python
1  def add(a, b):
2      return a + b  # Does not modify 'a' or 'b'
```

6. **Use Unit Testing**: Implement unit tests to ensure your functions are working correctly. This is especially important as your code becomes more complex.

```python
1  import unittest
2
3  class TestFunctions(unittest.TestCase):
4      def test_add(self):
5          self.assertEqual(add(2, 3), 5)
6
7  if __name__ == '__main__':
8      unittest.main()
```

Conclusion

The use of functions and modules is essential for writing clean, organized, and reusable code in Python. Functions allow us to encapsulate logic into manageable blocks, while modules facilitate the grouping of related functionalities. As we develop artificial intelligence systems and other projects, mastering these concepts will be crucial for maximizing code efficiency and readability. In light of these tools and approaches, we will be better equipped to tackle complex challenges in programming. In the next chapter, we will explore more complex and advanced data structures that will complement our programming skills.

## Chapter 11

Lists, Tuples, and Dictionaries

Introduction

In Python, as well as in other programming languages, data structures are a fundamental part that allows us to organize and manipulate information efficiently. Among the most commonly used data structures in Python are lists, tuples, and dictionaries. Each of these structures has its own characteristics and uses, and it is essential to understand them to build more efficient and readable programs. In this chapter, we will explore each of these structures, their properties, and how they are used in practical examples.

Lists

Definition

Lists are data structures that allow the storage of collections of elements in a specific order. They are mutable, which means they can be modified after their creation by adding, removing, or changing any of their elements. Lists can contain elements of different types, including numbers, strings, and even other lists.

Creating Lists

To create a list in Python, square brackets [] are used. Below is an example of how a list can be created:

```
1   fruits = ["apple", "banana", "cherry"]
```

In this example, we created a list called `fruits` that contains three elements: "apple," "banana," and "cherry."

Accessing Elements

Elements in a list can be accessed using indices. Indices in Python start from 0, which means the first element of the list has an index of 0.

```
1   first_fruit = fruits[0]  # "apple"
2   second_fruit = fruits[1]  # "banana"
```

Modifying Lists

Lists are mutable, meaning you can change their elements after they have been created. For example:

```
1  fruits[1] = "kiwi"  # Change "banana" to "kiwi"
```

Adding and Removing Elements

You can add elements to a list using the append() or insert() methods, and remove them using the remove() or pop() methods.

Adding elements:

```
1  fruits.append("orange")
      # Adds "orange" to the end of the list
2  fruits.insert(1, "strawberry")
      # Inserts "strawberry" at position 1
```

Removing elements:

```
1  fruits.remove("cherry")  # Removes "cherry" from the list
2  last_fruit = fruits.pop()
      # Removes the last element and returns it
```

Iterating over Lists

You can use a for loop to iterate through all the elements of a list:

```
1   for fruit in fruits:
2       print(fruit)
```

Practical Example with Lists

Suppose we want to maintain a shopping list. We can create, modify, and query our list using the operations described above:

```
1   shopping_list = []
2
3   # Adding elements
4   shopping_list.append("milk")
5   shopping_list.append("bread")
6   shopping_list.append("eggs")
7
8   # Modifying an element
9   shopping_list[1] = "whole grain bread"
10
11  # Removing an element
12  shopping_list.remove("eggs")
13
14  # Displaying the final list
15  print(shopping_list)  # Output: ['milk', 'whole grain bread']
```

Tuples

Definition

Tuples are very similar to lists, but they have a key difference: they are immutable. This means that once a tuple is created, no element can be changed, added, or removed. Due to their immutability, tuples are useful when it is necessary to ensure that data is not modified.

Creating Tuples

To create a tuple in Python, parentheses () are used:

```
1   coordinates = (10.0, 20.0)
```

Accessing Elements

Like with lists, elements in a tuple can be accessed using indices:

```
1   x = coordinates[0]  # 10.0
2   y = coordinates[1]  # 20.0
```

Attempting to Modify a Tuple

As mentioned earlier, tuples cannot be modified. Trying to change a value in a tuple will result in an error:

```
1   # This will raise an error
2   # coordinates[0] = 15.0
```

Iterating over Tuples

You can iterate over the elements of a tuple in the same way as you would with a list:

```
1  for coordinate in coordinates:
2      print(coordinate)
```

Practical Example with Tuples

Imagine we want to store the dimensions of a box (length, width, height) and ensure that these dimensions never change. We will use a tuple for this:

```
1  dimensions = (20, 15, 5)  # Length, width, height
2
3  # Displaying the dimensions
4  print(f"Length: {dimensions[0]}, Width: {dimensions[1]}
      , Height: {dimensions[2]}")
```

Dictionaries

Definition

Dictionaries are data structures that store key-value pairs. Like lists, they are mutable, meaning they can be modified. Dictionaries are ideal for storing data that can be accessed using a unique key.

Creating Dictionaries

To create a dictionary in Python, curly braces { } are used. Key-value pairs are separated by colons:

```
1   person = {"name": "John", "age": 30, "height": 1.75}
```

Accessing Elements

You can access values in a dictionary using their keys:

```
1   name = person["name"]   # "John"
2   age = person["age"]     # 30
```

Modifying Dictionaries

Values in a dictionary can be modified and added as follows:

```
1   person["age"] = 31      # Change the age
2   person["weight"] = 70   # Add a new field
```

Removing Elements

You can remove a key-value pair using the pop() method or del:

```
1   age = person.pop("age")
```

```
  # Removes "age" and returns its value
2 del person["height"]
  # Removes "height" from the dictionary
```

Iterating over Dictionaries

You can iterate through the keys or values of a dictionary using a `for` loop:

```
1  for key in person:
2      print(key, person[key])
   # Prints each key and its corresponding value
```

Practical Example with Dictionaries

Suppose we want to store information about a student. We can do this using a dictionary to maintain a clear relationship between the attributes:

```
1  student = {
2      "name": "Ana",
3      "age": 22,
4      "major": "Engineering"
5  }
6
7  # Displaying the student information
8  print(f"Name: {student['name']}, Age: {student['age']}
       , Major: {student['major']}")
```

Comparison of Lists, Tuples, and Dictionaries

Characteristic	Lists	Tuples	Dictionaries
Mutability	Mutable	Immutable	Mutable
Order	Yes	Yes	No (based on keys)
Access	By index	By index	By key
Common Use	Store collections of elements	Store immutable collections of data	Store key-value pairs

Conclusion

In this chapter, we explored the three most common data structures in Python: lists, tuples, and dictionaries. Each of these structures has its own purpose and specific characteristics, making them suitable for different types of tasks. By mastering the use of these structures, you will be able to manage and manipulate data more effectively, which is essential when developing artificial intelligence applications and other software. In the next chapter, we will cover sets and advanced data structures, further expanding our tools for efficient programming.

## Chapter 12

Sets and Advanced Data Structures

Introduction

In the world of programming, it is essential to select the appropriate data structure for each situation, as this can affect both code efficiency and clarity. While in previous chapters we explored lists, tuples, and dictionaries, in this chapter we will delve into sets and other advanced data structures. Sets are particularly useful when we need to manage collections of unique elements and perform mathematical operations like unions and intersections. Additionally, we will explore some advanced data structures such as stacks, queues, and trees, which provide us with more complex ways to organize and manipulate data.

Sets in Python

Definition

Sets are unordered and unindexed collections of unique elements. Due to their nature, they do not allow duplication of elements, making them ideal for operations that require checking for the existence of elements, as well as for removing duplicates from a list.

Creating Sets

To create a set in Python, we use the `set()` function, or we can use curly braces `{}`. Below is a basic example of how to create a set:

```python
fruit_set = {"apple", "banana", "cherry"}
```

We can also create a set from a list:

```python
fruit_list = ["apple", "banana", "cherry", "apple"]
fruit_set = set(fruit_list)  # Removes duplicates
print(fruit_set)  # Output: {'apple', 'banana', 'cherry'}
```

Set Operations

Sets in Python allow us to perform various mathematical operations easily and efficiently, including union, intersection, and difference.

Union

The union of two sets combines all the unique elements of both. This can be done using the | operator or the `union()` method:

```python
set1 = {1, 2, 3}
set2 = {3, 4, 5}
union = set1 | set2
print(union)  # Output: {1, 2, 3, 4, 5}
```

Intersection

The intersection returns only the elements that are present in both sets. It can be performed with the & operator or the `intersection()` method:

```python
intersection = set1 & set2
print(intersection)  # Output: {3}
```

Difference

The difference returns the elements that are in the first set but not in the second. It can be done with the − operator or the `difference()` method:

```python
difference = set1 - set2
print(difference)  # Output: {1, 2}
```

Symmetric Difference

The symmetric difference returns the elements that are in one of the sets but not in both. It can be done with the ^ operator or the symmetric_difference() method:

```
1  symmetric_difference = set1 ^ set2
2  print(symmetric_difference)  # Output: {1, 2, 4, 5}
```

Useful Set Methods

Sets also have several useful methods:

- add(element): Adds an element to the set.

- remove(element): Removes an element from the set. Raises an error if the element is not present.

- discard(element): Similar to remove(), but does not raise an error if the element does not exist.

- clear(): Removes all elements from the set.

```
1  fruit_set.add("orange")
2  print(fruit_set)
     # Output: {'apple', 'banana', 'cherry', 'orange'}
3
4  fruit_set.remove("banana")
5  print(fruit_set)  # Output: {'apple', 'cherry', 'orange'}
```

Advanced Data Structures

Stacks

A stack is a data structure that follows the LIFO (Last In, First Out) principle, meaning that the last element added is the first one to be removed. Stacks can be used in various applications, such as managing undo/redo in text editors or for expression evaluation.

Creating and Using Stacks

Although Python does not have a built-in stack data type, we can implement a stack using lists. Below is a simple example:

```python
stack = []

# Add elements to the stack
stack.append("first")
stack.append("second")
stack.append("third")

# Remove elements from the stack
last_element = stack.pop()  # "third"
print(last_element)  # Output: third
```

Queues

A queue is a data structure that operates on the FIFO (First In, First Out) principle. That is, the first element added is the first one to be removed.

Queues are useful in programming scenarios that require managing tasks in a specific order, such as in print systems or process management.

Creating and Using Queues

Like stacks, queues can be implemented using lists, though for more efficient performance, the `collections` module in Python is preferred.

```python
from collections import deque

queue = deque()

# Add elements to the queue
queue.append("first")
queue.append("second")
queue.append("third")

# Remove elements from the queue
first_element = queue.popleft()  # "first"
print(first_element)  # Output: first
```

Trees

Trees are more complex data structures that consist of nodes connected by edges. A tree has a root node, and each node may have zero or more child nodes. Trees are commonly used in databases and in the representation of hierarchies.

Introduction to Trees

A common type of tree is the binary tree, where each node has at most two children (called the left child and the right child). Trees can be used to organize data efficiently, allowing for fast searches, insertions, and deletions.

```python
1   class Node:
2       def __init__(self, value):
3           self.value = value
4           self.left = None
5           self.right = None
6
7   class BinaryTree:
8       def __init__(self):
9           self.root = None
10
11      def add(self, value):
12          if self.root is None:
13              self.root = Node(value)
14          else:
15              self._add(value, self.root)
16
17      def _add(self, value, current_node):
18          if value < current_node.value:
19              if current_node.left is None:
20                  current_node.left = Node(value)
21              else:
22                  self._add(value, current_node.left)
23          else:
24              if current_node.right is None:
25                  current_node.right = Node(value)
26              else:
27                  self._add(value, current_node.right)
28
29  # Create a tree and add elements
30  tree = BinaryTree()
31  tree.add(10)
```

```
32  tree.add(5)
33  tree.add(15)
```

Comparison of Data Structures

Data Structure	Purpose	Mutability	Order
Lists	Store ordered collections	Mutable	Yes
Tuples	Store immutable collections	Immutable	Yes
Dictionaries	Store key-value pairs	Mutable	No
Sets	Store unique elements	Mutable	No
Stacks	LIFO management	Mutable	No
Queues	FIFO management	Mutable	No
Trees	Hierarchical organization	Mutable	No

Conclusion

In this chapter, we explored sets and various advanced data structures such as stacks, queues, and trees. By understanding the differences and applications of each of these structures, you will be able to select the appropriate one to solve specific problems more efficiently. These tools are fundamental for building algorithms and applications in artificial intelligence that require effective data management. In the next chapter, we will delve into sorting and searching algorithms, equipping you with more knowledge to manipulate and manage data in your projects.

## Chapter 13

Introduction to Algorithm Complexity

Introduction

When working with algorithms and data structures, it is crucial to understand not just how they work, but also how they behave in terms of efficiency as input sizes increase. This is where the concept of algorithm complexity comes into play. The complexity of an algorithm refers to the amount of resources that an algorithm consumes, whether time (time complexity) or space (space complexity). This chapter will primarily focus on the time complexity of algorithms, using Big O notation as a key tool to describe and compare the efficiency of different approaches.

Big O Notation

Big O notation is a mathematical way to describe the complexity of an algorithm in relation to the size of the input (n). This notation allows us to classify algorithms based on their performance in the worst case, facilitating comparison between different algorithms.

Concept

Big O notation is used to describe the growth rate of an algorithm's complexity in relation to input sizes. This means it focuses on how an algorithm behaves as the size of the data increases, ignoring constants and lower-order terms. Thus, we say that an algorithm has a complexity of $O(f(n))$ if there exist constants C and n_0 such that for all $n > n_0$, the complexity of the algorithm is at most $C*f(n)$.

Examples of Big O Notation

- **O(1)**: Constant complexity. The execution time does not change with the size of the input. For example, accessing an element from a list using an index.

```
1   def get_first_element(lst):
2       return lst[0]   # Constant access
```

- **O(n)**: Linear complexity. The execution time increases linearly with the size of the input. For example, searching for an element in a list.

```
1   def linear_search(lst, target):
```

```
2        for element in lst:
3            if element == target:
4                return True
5        return False  # Requires O(n) in the worst case
```

- **O(n^2)**: Quadratic complexity. The execution time increases quadratically with the size of the input. This often occurs in simple sorting algorithms, such as bubble sort.

```
1  def bubble_sort(lst):
2      n = len(lst)
3      for i in range(n):
4          for j in range(0, n-i-1):
5              if lst[j] > lst[j+1]:
6                  lst[j], lst[j+1] = lst[j+1], lst[j]
```

- **O(log n)**: Logarithmic complexity. Indicates that the execution time grows logarithmically with the size of the input. This occurs, for example, in binary search algorithms.

```
1  def binary_search(lst, target):
2      low, high = 0, len(lst) - 1
3      while low <= high:
4          mid = (low + high) // 2
5          if lst[mid] == target:
6              return mid
7          elif lst[mid] < target:
8              low = mid + 1
9          else:
10             high = mid - 1
11     return -1
```

- **O(n log n)**: This is typical of efficient sorting algorithms like Merge

Sort and Quick Sort.

```python
1   def merge_sort(lst):
2       if len(lst) <= 1:
3           return lst
4       mid = len(lst) // 2
5       left = merge_sort(lst[:mid])
6       right = merge_sort(lst[mid:])
7       return merge(left, right)
8
9   def merge(lst1, lst2):
10      result = []
11      i = j = 0
12      while i < len(lst1) and j < len(lst2):
13          if lst1[i] < lst2[j]:
14              result.append(lst1[i])
15              i += 1
16          else:
17              result.append(lst2[j])
18              j += 1
19      result.extend(lst1[i:])
20      result.extend(lst2[j:])
21      return result
```

Complexity Analysis

Analyzing the complexity of an algorithm involves evaluating how much time and space it requires as the input size changes. This is typically done through systematic steps, assessing the number of basic operations performed.

Steps to Analyze Time Complexity

1. **Identify the most expensive operation**: Determine which step is the most costly within the algorithm. This is rarely the initialization step and is usually a loop or a nested operation.

2. **Count operations**: Count how many operations are performed based on the input size (n). Some examples include comparisons, assignments, and arithmetic calculations.

3. **Find the relationship**: If there are nested loops, the complexity of the algorithm can become $O(n^2)$ or even $O(n^3)$. So, while counting the operations, they can be grouped.

4. **Simplify using Big O Notation**: The final step is to express the result in Big O notation, ignoring constants and lower-order terms.

Practical Example of Analysis

Consider a simple algorithm that sums all the elements of a list:

```python
def sum_list(lst):
    total = 0
    for number in lst:
        total += number
    return total
```

Analysis

1. **Identify the most expensive operation**: The most expensive operation here is the loop that iterates through the list.

2. **Count operations**: If we have n elements in the list, the loop will execute n times.

3. **Find the relationship**: There are n additions performed in the worst case.

4. **Simplify**: The complexity of this algorithm is O(n).

Example of Quadratic Complexity

Now, consider an algorithm that prints many pairs from a list:

```python
def print_pairs(lst):
    for i in range(len(lst)):
        for j in range(len(lst)):
            print(lst[i], lst[j])
```

Analysis

1. **Identify the most expensive operation**: The nested loops are the most costly.

2. **Count operations**: The nested loops run n times each, i.e., a total of n * n = n².

3. **Find the relationship**: The complexity of this algorithm is O(n²).

4. **Simplify**: Given that there are constants involved, it is simply expressed as O(n²).

Space Complexity

While time complexity is the most commonly discussed, space complexity also needs consideration, referring to the amount of additional memory that the algorithm requires based on input size.

Examples of Space Complexity

- **O(1)**: This is constant space complexity, where no additional space is required beyond the variables used.

- **O(n)**: In this case, additional space proportional to the size of the input is used, such as storing all elements in a list or array.

Conclusion

Understanding the complexity of algorithms is essential for developers and data scientists looking to build efficient systems. By using Big O notation, we can clearly communicate how an algorithm behaves in terms of time and space, allowing informed decisions when selecting the best approach to solve a specific problem. With this foundation, the next step will be to explore optimization techniques to further improve the efficiency of our algorithms and learn to apply these concepts to real-world problems in artificial intelligence.

## Chapter 14

Sorting and Searching Algorithms

Introduction

The study of sorting and searching algorithms is fundamental in programming and data science, particularly in the field of artificial intelligence. The ability to efficiently organize and retrieve data is at the heart of almost all computer applications. This chapter will focus on various sorting algorithms, their characteristics, advantages, and disadvantages, and will explore search methods necessary to locate information within a collection of data.

Sorting Algorithms

Sorting is the process of rearranging the elements of a collection, such as a list or an array, according to a specific order, either ascending or descending. There are several sorting algorithms, and although their efficiency may vary, most are comparable in terms of time complexity. Below, we will explore some of the most well-known sorting algorithms.

Bubble Sort

The bubble sort algorithm is one of the simplest and least efficient methods. Its operation consists of comparing each pair of adjacent elements in a list and, if they are in the wrong order, swapping them. This process is repeated until no more swaps are made, indicating that the list is sorted.

Implementation

```
1   def bubble_sort(arr):
2       n = len(arr)
3       for i in range(n):
4           for j in range(0, n-i-1):
5               if arr[j] > arr[j+1]:
6                   arr[j], arr[j+1] = arr[j+1], arr[j]
7       return arr
8
9   # Example usage
10  numbers = [64, 34, 25, 12, 22, 11, 90]
11  print(bubble_sort(numbers))
    # Output: [11, 12, 22, 25, 34, 64, 90]
```

Complexity Analysis

- **Time Complexity**: O(n^2) in the worst and average cases.

- **Space Complexity**: O(1) since it performs the sorting in place.

Selection Sort

Similar to bubble sort, the selection sort algorithm sorts a list iteratively, but it does so in a slightly different way. In each iteration, it searches for the smallest value in the unsorted portion of the list and swaps it with the first unsorted element.

Implementation

```
1   def selection_sort(arr):
2       n = len(arr)
3       for i in range(n):
4           min_index = i
5           for j in range(i+1, n):
6               if arr[j] < arr[min_index]:
7                   min_index = j
8           arr[i], arr[min_index] = arr[min_index], arr[i]
9       return arr
10
11  # Example usage
12  numbers = [64, 34, 25, 12, 22, 11, 90]
13  print(selection_sort(numbers))
    # Output: [11, 12, 22, 25, 34, 64, 90]
```

Complexity Analysis

- **Time Complexity**: O(n^2) in all cases.
- **Space Complexity**: O(1).

Insertion Sort

The insertion sort algorithm builds the sorted list one element at a time, taking an element from the unsorted list and placing it in its correct position within the sorted list.

Implementation

```
1   def insertion_sort(arr):
2       for i in range(1, len(arr)):
3           key = arr[i]
4           j = i - 1
5           while j >= 0 and key < arr[j]:
6               arr[j + 1] = arr[j]
7               j -= 1
8           arr[j + 1] = key
9       return arr
10
11  # Example usage
12  numbers = [64, 34, 25, 12, 22, 11, 90]
13  print(insertion_sort(numbers))
    # Output: [11, 12, 22, 25, 34, 64, 90]
```

Complexity Analysis

- **Time Complexity**: O(n^2) in the worst and average cases, O(n) in the best case (already sorted list).

- **Space Complexity**: O(1).

Merge Sort

Unlike the previous methods, Merge Sort is an efficient sorting algorithm that uses a "divide and conquer" approach. This algorithm divides the list in half, recursively sorts each half, and then merges the sorted halves.

Implementation

```python
1   def merge(list1, list2):
2       result = []
3       i = j = 0
4       while i < len(list1) and j < len(list2):
5           if list1[i] < list2[j]:
6               result.append(list1[i])
7               i += 1
8           else:
9               result.append(list2[j])
10              j += 1
11      result.extend(list1[i:])
12      result.extend(list2[j:])
13      return result
14
15  def merge_sort(arr):
16      if len(arr) <= 1:
17          return arr
18      mid = len(arr) // 2
19      left = merge_sort(arr[:mid])
20      right = merge_sort(arr[mid:])
21      return merge(left, right)
22
23  # Example usage
24  numbers = [64, 34, 25, 12, 22, 11, 90]
```

```
25  print(merge_sort(numbers))
    # Output: [11, 12, 22, 25, 34, 64, 90]
```

Complexity Analysis

- **Time Complexity**: O(n log n) in all cases.

- **Space Complexity**: O(n) due to the creation of temporary lists during the merge.

Quick Sort

Quick sort is another efficient sorting algorithm that, like Merge Sort, also employs a "divide and conquer" approach. It selects a "pivot" and moves elements smaller than the pivot to one side and larger ones to the other. It then recursively applies the same process to the sublists.

Implementation

```
1  def quick_sort(arr):
2      if len(arr) <= 1:
3          return arr
4      pivot = arr[0]
5      less_than_pivot = [x for x in arr[1:] if x <= pivot]
6      greater_than_pivot = [x for x in arr[1:] if x > pivot]
7      return quick_sort(less_than_pivot) + [pivot] +
   quick_sort(greater_than_pivot)
8
9  # Example usage
10 numbers = [64, 34, 25, 12, 22, 11, 90]
```

```
11  print(quick_sort(numbers))
    # Output: [11, 12, 22, 25, 34, 64, 90]
```

Complexity Analysis

- **Time Complexity**: O(n^2) in the worst case, O(n log n) in the average case.

- **Space Complexity**: O(log n) in the average case.

Comparison of Sorting Algorithms

Algorithm	Best Case	Average Case	Worst Case	Space Complexity
Bubble Sort	O(n)	O(n^2)	O(n^2)	O(1)
Selection Sort	O(n^2)	O(n^2)	O(n^2)	O(1)
Insertion Sort	O(n)	O(n^2)	O(n^2)	O(1)
Merge Sort	O(n log n)	O(n log n)	O(n log n)	O(n)
Quick Sort	O(n log n)	O(n log n)	O(n^2)	O(log n)

Searching Algorithms

Once data is sorted, it can be searched more efficiently. Searching algorithms are essential for retrieving data from lists or arrays. We will examine two popular techniques: linear search and binary search.

Linear Search

Linear search is the simplest method. It consists of traversing each element of the list until the desired value is found. It is efficient for small lists but is not recommended for large lists due to its complexity.

Implementation

```python
def linear_search(arr, target):
    for index, value in enumerate(arr):
        if value == target:
            return index
    return -1

# Example usage
numbers = [64, 34, 25, 12, 22, 11, 90]
result = linear_search(numbers, 22)
print("Element found at position:", result)
    # Output: Element found at position: 4
```

Complexity Analysis

- **Time Complexity**: O(n).
- **Space Complexity**: O(1).

Binary Search

Binary search is a much more efficient method that only applies to sorted lists. It repeatedly divides the list in half, eliminating the half that cannot contain the target. This process is repeated until the element is found or the search is reduced to zero.

Implementation

```
1  def binary_search(arr, target):
2      start = 0
3      end = len(arr) - 1
4      while start <= end:
5          mid = (start + end) // 2
6          if arr[mid] == target:
7              return mid
8          elif arr[mid] < target:
9              start = mid + 1
10         else:
11             end = mid - 1
12     return -1
13
14 # Example usage
15 numbers = [11, 12, 22, 25, 34, 64, 90]
16 result = binary_search(numbers, 22)
17 print("Element found at position:", result)
   # Output: Element found at position: 2
```

Complexity Analysis

- **Time Complexity**: O(log n).

- **Space Complexity**: O(1).

Comparison of Searching Algorithms

Algorithm	Best Time Complexity	Average Time Complexity	Worst Time Complexity	Space Complexity
Linear Search	O(1)	O(n)	O(n)	O(1)
Binary Search	O(1)	O(log n)	O(log n)	O(1)

Conclusion

This chapter has reviewed various sorting and searching algorithms, highlighting that each algorithm has its own set of advantages and disadvantages. Choosing the right algorithm depends on factors such as the size of the data collection, its specific characteristics, and the need for time and space efficiency. By mastering these concepts, you will be well-equipped to tackle more complex problems in artificial intelligence and other areas of programming.

## Chapter 15

Reading and Writing Files in Python

Introduction

In the world of programming, working with data is not limited to just manipulating it in memory; often, we need to read data from files or save results into them for later use. The ability to read and write files is a fundamental skill that every programmer should master. In this chapter, we will explore how Python handles file input and output, addressing key concepts such as handling text files, as well as files in more structured formats like CSV and JSON. We will also discuss how to implement effective exception handling to ensure that our programs are robust and resistant to common errors.

Handling Text Files

Opening Files

To work with files in Python, we first need to open them using the `open()` function. This function takes at least one argument: the name of the file we want to open. We can also specify a mode of opening, which determines how we will interact with the file. Common modes are:

- `r`: Read mode (default). Opens the file and allows reading its content.

- `w`: Write mode. Creates a new file if it does not exist, or truncates (deletes) the existing content if it does.

- `a`: Append mode. Opens the file and allows adding content to the end without deleting existing content.

- `b`: Binary mode. Can be combined with other modes to work with binary files.

Below is an example of how to open a file in read mode:

```
file = open('my_file.txt', 'r')
```

Reading Files

Once the file is opened, we can read its content. There are several ways to do this:

Read the whole content

To read the entire content of the file at once, we use the `read()` method.

```
1  content = file.read()
2  print(content)
```

Read line by line

If the file is large or we wish to process it line by line, we can use `readline()` or `readlines()`. The `readline()` method reads one line at a time, while `readlines()` reads all lines and returns them as a list.

```
1  # Read line by line
2  line = file.readline()
3  while line:
4      print(line)
5      line = file.readline()
6
7  # Or read all lines into a list
8  lines = file.readlines()
9  for line in lines:
10     print(line)
```

Writing to Files

To write to a file, we first open it in write (`w`) or append (`a`) mode. If we open a file in write mode and it already exists, its content will be erased. To avoid this, we can use append mode, which adds new content to the end of the file.

```
1  write_file = open('my_file.txt', 'w')
2  write_file.write('Hello, world!\n')
3  write_file.write('Writing to a file from Python.\n')
4  write_file.close()
```

Closing Files

It is very important to close the file once the operations are finished to free up system resources. This is done with the `close()` method.

```
1  file.close()
```

However, in Python, it is recommended to use the `with` context, which ensures that the file is closed automatically once the operations are completed, even if an error occurs:

```
1  with open('my_file.txt', 'r') as file:
2      content = file.read()
3      print(content)
```

Exception Handling

When working with files, it is important to handle exceptions, as errors can occur such as a file not being found or permission issues. We can use `try` and `except` blocks to manage these errors in a controlled manner.

```
1  try:
```

```
2      with open('my_file.txt', 'r') as file:
3          content = file.read()
4  except FileNotFoundError:
5      print("The file was not found.")
6  except PermissionError:
7      print("You do not have permission to access this file.")
```

CSV Files

One of the most common file formats for storing tabular data is CSV (Comma-Separated Values). This format allows storing information in text form, using commas to separate each value. Python provides a built-in library called `csv` that makes handling CSV files easier.

Reading CSV Files

```
1  import csv
2
3  with open('data.csv', 'r') as csv_file:
4      reader = csv.reader(csv_file)
5      for row in reader:
6          print(row)
```

Writing to CSV Files

To write to a CSV file, we use `csv.writer()`. This object provides a convenient way to add rows to a file.

```
1   import csv
2
3   data = [
4       ['Name', 'Age', 'City'],
5       ['John', 25, 'Madrid'],
6       ['Anna', 30, 'Barcelona'],
7       ['Luis', 40, 'Valencia']
8   ]
9
10  with open('output.csv', 'w', newline='') as csv_file:
11      writer = csv.writer(csv_file)
12      writer.writerows(data)
```

JSON Files

The JSON (JavaScript Object Notation) format is another popular standard for storing data, especially when working with structured data. Python includes the json module to facilitate the manipulation of JSON files.

Reading JSON Files

```
1   import json
2
3   with open('data.json', 'r') as json_file:
4       data = json.load(json_file)
5       print(data)
```

Writing to JSON Files

To write to a JSON file, we use `json.dump()`.

```
1   import json
2
3   data = {
4       "name": "John",
5       "age": 25,
6       "city": "Madrid"
7   }
8
9   with open('output.json', 'w') as json_file:
10      json.dump(data, json_file, indent=4)
```

Conclusion

In this chapter, we have covered the fundamentals of reading and writing files in Python, including text files, CSV, and JSON. We learned how to open, read, write, and close files, as well as the importance of handling exceptions to create more robust programs. Mastering these techniques will not only help us work with data efficiently but is also essential for building more complex applications in artificial intelligence. As we move forward, these concepts will become crucial tools in our programming arsenal. In the next chapter, we will focus on the use of relational databases with Python, delving into the storage and retrieval of large amounts of data.

## Chapter 16

Using Relational Databases with Python

Introduction

In application development, it is common to need to store and retrieve large amounts of data in a structured and efficient way. Relational databases are a popular option for handling this task, as they allow data to be organized in tables and establish relationships between them. In this chapter, we will explore how to interact with relational databases using Python, focusing on the `sqlite3` library that comes bundled with Python and `SQLAlchemy`, a very popular ORM (Object Relational Mapper) that simplifies interactions with databases.

What is a Relational Database

A relational database is a data storage system that organizes information into tables that can be linked to each other. Each table consists of rows (tuples) and columns (attributes) that provide structured and organized access to the data. Relational databases use SQL (Structured Query Language) to perform queries and manipulate information.

Installation and Setup

Before getting started, make sure you have Python installed on your system. The `sqlite3` library is included by default, so you do not need any additional installation. For `SQLAlchemy`, you can install it using the package manager `pip`:

```
1    pip install sqlalchemy
```

Connecting to the Database

Using sqlite3

The `sqlite3` library allows developers to create and manage SQLite databases. Below, we will show how to establish a connection to a database and create a table.

```
1    import sqlite3
2
```

```
3   # Connect to or create a database
4   connection = sqlite3.connect('my_data.db')
5   cursor = connection.cursor()
6
7   # Create a table
8   cursor.execute('''
9   CREATE TABLE IF NOT EXISTS users (
10      id INTEGER PRIMARY KEY AUTOINCREMENT,
11      name TEXT NOT NULL,
12      age INTEGER NOT NULL
13  )
14  ''')
15
16  # Commit the changes
17  connection.commit()
18
19  # Close the connection
20  connection.close()
```

Using SQLAlchemy

`SQLAlchemy` provides a more abstract and robust way to interact with databases. First, we will import the necessary classes and perform the initial setup.

```
1   from sqlalchemy import create_engine, Column, Integer,
    String
2   from sqlalchemy.ext.declarative import declarative_base
3   from sqlalchemy.orm import sessionmaker
4
5   # Create an SQLite database
6   engine = create_engine('sqlite:///my_data.db')
7   Base = declarative_base()
```

```
 8
 9   # Define a user model
10   class User(Base):
11       __tablename__ = 'users'
12       id = Column(Integer, primary_key=True, autoincrement=
     True)
13       name = Column(String, nullable=False)
14       age = Column(Integer, nullable=False)
15
16   # Create all tables
17   Base.metadata.create_all(engine)
18
19   # Establish the session
20   Session = sessionmaker(bind=engine)
21   session = Session()
```

CRUD Operations

CRUD operations (Create, Read, Update, Delete) are fundamental for manipulating data in a database. Below, each of these operations is detailed:

Create (Insert Data)

Using sqlite3

Let's add some records to our users table.

```
1   connection = sqlite3.connect('my_data.db')
```

```
 2  cursor = connection.cursor()
 3
 4  # Insert data
 5  cursor.execute("INSERT INTO users (name, age) VALUES (?, ?)",
        ('John', 28))
 6  cursor.execute("INSERT INTO users (name, age) VALUES (?, ?)",
        ('Anna', 24))
 7
 8  # Commit changes
 9  connection.commit()
10  connection.close()
```

Using SQLAlchemy

```
 1  # Create new users
 2  new_user1 = User(name='John', age=28)
 3  new_user2 = User(name='Anna', age=24)
 4
 5  # Add users to the session and save changes
 6  session.add(new_user1)
 7  session.add(new_user2)
 8  session.commit()
```

Read (Query Data)

To read data from a database, we can perform queries using SQL.

Using sqlite3

```
1  connection = sqlite3.connect('my_data.db')
2  cursor = connection.cursor()
3
4  # Query data
5  cursor.execute("SELECT * FROM users")
6  users = cursor.fetchall()
7
8  for user in users:
9      print(user)
10
11 connection.close()
```

Using SQLAlchemy

```
1  # Read all users
2  users = session.query(User).all()
3
4  for user in users:
5      print(user.name, user.age)
```

Update (Modify Data)

Using sqlite3

```
1  connection = sqlite3.connect('my_data.db')
2  cursor = connection.cursor()
3
4  # Update 'John's record
5  cursor.execute("UPDATE users SET age = ? WHERE name = ?", (29
   , 'John'))
6
7  connection.commit()
8  connection.close()
```

Using SQLAlchemy

```
1  # Update the age of user 'John'
2  user_j = session.query(User).filter_by(name='John').first()
3  user_j.age = 29
4
5  session.commit()
```

Delete (Remove Data)

Using sqlite3

```
1  connection = sqlite3.connect('my_data.db')
2  cursor = connection.cursor()
3
4  # Delete a user
5  cursor.execute("DELETE FROM users WHERE name = ?", ('Anna',))
6
7  connection.commit()
8  connection.close()
```

Using SQLAlchemy

```
1  # Delete user 'Anna'
2  user_a = session.query(User).filter_by(name='Anna').first()
3  session.delete(user_a)
4
5  session.commit()
```

Error and Exception Handling

When performing operations on databases, it is critical to handle exceptions to ensure the stability and integrity of the application. We can use `try` and `except` blocks to catch common errors, such as connection failures or data integrity issues.

```
1  try:
2      connection = sqlite3.connect('my_data.db')
3      cursor = connection.cursor()
4      cursor.execute(
       "INSERT INTO users (name, age) VALUES (?, ?)", ('Carlos',
       30))
5      connection.commit()
6  except sqlite3.Error as e:
7      print("Error interacting with the database: ", e)
8  finally:
9      if connection:
10         connection.close()
```

Advanced Queries

With both sqlite3 and SQLAlchemy, we can perform more complex queries, such as filtering, sorting, and joining tables. Below are a couple of examples.

Data Filtering

```
1  # Using sqlite3
2  cursor.execute("SELECT * FROM users WHERE age > 25")
3  older_users = cursor.fetchall()
```

```
1  # Using SQLAlchemy
2  older_users = session.query(User).filter(User.age > 25).all()
```

Data Sorting

```
1  # Using sqlite3
2  cursor.execute("SELECT * FROM users ORDER BY age ASC")
3  sorted_users = cursor.fetchall()
```

```
1  # Using SQLAlchemy
2  sorted_users = session.query(User).order_by(User.age.asc()).
   all()
```

Conclusion

Throughout this chapter, we have explored how to manage relational databases using Python. From establishing a connection and performing CRUD operations to handling errors and conducting advanced queries, we have covered the essential aspects of effectively interacting with databases. Understanding these skills is fundamental for any developer looking to build robust and efficient applications, many of which are crucial in artificial intelligence projects. With this foundation, you will be prepared to explore more complex databases and advanced techniques in future volumes of this series.

## Chapter 17

Introduction to NoSQL Databases

Introduction

In today's information technology ecosystem, traditional (relational) databases have been the norm for decades. However, with the evolution of applications and more complex data needs, an alternative has emerged known as NoSQL databases (Not Only SQL). This chapter will explore what NoSQL databases are, their characteristics, types, advantages, disadvantages, and how to interact with them using Python.

What are NoSQL Databases?

NoSQL databases are database management systems that differ from traditional relational databases in their structure, data model, and capabilities. Their design focuses on horizontal scalability and flexibility, allowing for the storage and processing of unstructured or semi-structured data.

Unlike SQL databases, which use tables and strict relationships, NoSQL databases can store data in various formats, including documents, key-value pairs, columns, and graphs. This allows developers to manage data in a more agile and adaptive manner, especially in web applications, big data, and distributed systems.

Types of NoSQL Databases

There are several types of NoSQL databases, each designed to meet different needs and use cases. Below, we review the most prominent types:

Document Databases

These databases store information in flexible documents, which generally use the JSON (JavaScript Object Notation) format. Each document can contain multiple fields and nested structures, allowing for a richer data organization. MongoDB is one of the most recognized examples of document databases.

Example:

```
1  {
2      "name": "John",
3      "age": 28,
4      "city": "Madrid",
5      "interests": ["programming", "soccer", "music"]
6  }
```

Key-Value Databases

This type of database stores data as key-value pairs. Each item can be retrieved using its unique key. This model is simple and provides quick access to the data. Redis and Amazon DynamoDB are examples of this type of database.

Example:

Key	Value
"user_1"	{"name": "John", "age": 28}
"user_2"	{"name": "Ana", "age": 24}

Column Databases

Column databases store data in columns instead of rows. This model is very efficient for performing read and write operations on large volumes of data. Apache Cassandra and HBase are known for this approach.

Example:

Name	Age	City
John	28	Madrid
Ana	24	Barcelona

Graph Databases

These systems are designed to store and manipulate data that is intricately interconnected. They use nodes, edges, and properties to represent and store data. Neo4j is a popular example in this field.

Example:

- Node: John

- Node: Ana

- Edge: Friend of

Comparison of NoSQL Database Types

Type of Database	Structure	Example Use
Document	JSON, BSON	Web applications, CMS
Key-Value	Key-value pairs	Caching, sessions
Column	Columns and rows	Big data analysis
Graph	Nodes and relationships	Social networks, recommendations

Advantages of NoSQL Databases

NoSQL databases offer several advantages over their relational counterparts:

1. **Horizontal Scalability**: They allow you to add more machines to distribute load and data, improving performance more efficiently.

2. **Flexibility in Data Model**: They support unstructured data formats and facilitate adaptation to changes in schemas.

3. **High Performance**: Optimized for fast read and write operations, which is beneficial for real-time applications.

4. **Handling Massive Data**: Suitable for managing large volumes of data without requiring alignment with a fixed schema.

Disadvantages of NoSQL Databases

However, there are also disadvantages that must be considered:

1. **Lack of Standards**: Unlike SQL, which is a defined standard, NoSQL lacks a standardized query language, which can hinder portability.

2. **Eventual Consistency**: Many NoSQL databases employ an eventual consistency model, which could be an issue for applications where data integrity is crucial.

3. **Fewer Management Tools**: NoSQL databases often have fewer tools available for tasks such as data migration or user management.

Installation and Configuration of MongoDB

Next, we will show how to install and configure MongoDB, one of the most popular NoSQL databases.

Installation

To install MongoDB, you can use your operating system's package manager or download the installer from the official website. Here's an example of installation using `apt` for Debian-based systems:

```
1  sudo apt update
2  sudo apt install -y mongodb
```

Configuration

After installation, you can start the MongoDB server:

```
1  sudo systemctl start mongodb
2  sudo systemctl enable mongodb
```

Interacting with MongoDB

To interact with MongoDB, we will use the `pymongo` library. First, you need to install it:

```
1  pip install pymongo
```

Connecting to MongoDB

Here's how to connect to your MongoDB database using Python:

```
1   from pymongo import MongoClient
2
3   # Connect to the local MongoDB server
4   client = MongoClient('localhost', 27017)
5
6   # Create or access a database called 'my_database'
7   db = client['my_database']
8
9   # Create or access a collection called 'users'
10  collection = db['users']
```

Inserting Documents

To insert documents into your collection, we use the `insert_one` or `insert_many` methods:

```
1   # Insert a single document
2   user = {
3       "name": "John",
4       "age": 28,
5       "city": "Madrid"
6   }
7   collection.insert_one(user)
8
9   # Insert multiple documents
10  users = [
11      {"name": "Ana", "age": 24, "city": "Barcelona"},
12      {"name": "Luis", "age": 30, "city": "Valencia"}
13  ]
14  collection.insert_many(users)
```

Querying Documents

To query documents from the database:

```
1   # Retrieve all users
2   all_users = collection.find()
3
4   for user in all_users:
5       print(user)
6
7   # Retrieve users that meet conditions
```

```
8  older_users = collection.find({"age": {"$gt": 25}})
     # Users older than 25
9  for user in older_users:
10     print(user)
```

Updating Documents

To update documents, you can use the update_one and update_many methods:

```
1  # Update John's age
2  collection.update_one({"name": "John"}, {"$set": {"age": 29}}
     )
3
4  # Increment the age of all users by 1
5  collection.update_many({}, {"$inc": {"age": 1}})
```

Deleting Documents

Document deletion can be done using delete_one or delete_many:

```
1  # Delete a document
2  collection.delete_one({"name": "Ana"})
3
4  # Delete all users under 25
5  collection.delete_many({"age": {"$lt": 25}})
```

Conclusion

NoSQL databases have revolutionized the way we manage and manipulate data, offering flexibility and scalability that are necessary in many modern applications. This chapter has explored the different types of NoSQL databases, their advantages and disadvantages, and how to interact with MongoDB using Python. By understanding these concepts, you will be better prepared to face the challenges associated with data management in the fields of artificial intelligence and contemporary application development. In the next chapter, we will address advanced techniques in artificial intelligence, where effective data manipulation will be an invaluable resource.

## Chapter 18

Introduction to NumPy

Introduction

NumPy is one of the most fundamental and essential libraries in Python for data science and data analysis. It is a powerful library for performing numerical computations and is particularly known for its efficiency in manipulating arrays and multidimensional matrices. In this chapter, we will explore what NumPy is, how to install it, and how to use its main features to facilitate the manipulation and analysis of numerical data.

What is NumPy?

NumPy, which stands for "Numerical Python," is a library that offers support for large, multidimensional arrays and matrices, along with a collection of high-level mathematical functions to operate on these arrays. NumPy is widely used in data science, machine learning, and image processing, among other fields.

Advantages of Using NumPy

1. **Speed**: NumPy allows vectorized operations, meaning it can perform operations on entire arrays at once, rather than using loops to iterate through elements. This results in much faster execution.

2. **Lower memory usage**: NumPy uses a more efficient storage format for its arrays compared to standard Python lists, allowing for more comfortable handling of large amounts of data.

3. **Mathematical functions**: It comes with a wide variety of mathematical, statistical, and linear algebra functions that facilitate data analysis.

4. **Integration with other libraries**: NumPy easily integrates with other popular libraries such as Pandas, Matplotlib, and SciPy, which are foundational tools in data science.

Installing NumPy

To start using NumPy, we first need to install it. If you have Python installed, you can do this using the package manager `pip`. Let's open a terminal or command line and execute the following command:

```
1  pip install numpy
```

Once installed, we can verify the installation by opening a Python console or script and executing:

```
1  import numpy as np
2
```

```
3  print(np.__version__)
```

This will display the installed version of NumPy, confirming that the installation was successful.

Creating Arrays with NumPy

The central feature of NumPy is its arrays, which are list-like objects that can contain numbers but can also be more complex, such as matrices or tensors.

Creating a One-Dimensional Array

We can create a one-dimensional array (vector) using the `np.array()` function:

```
1  import numpy as np
2
3  one_dimensional_array = np.array([1, 2, 3, 4, 5])
4  print(one_dimensional_array)
```

Creating a Two-Dimensional Array

To create a two-dimensional array (matrix), we simply pass a list of lists to `np.array()`:

```
1  two_dimensional_array = np.array([[1, 2, 3], [4, 5, 6]])
2  print(two_dimensional_array)
```

Generating Arrays with Specialized Functions

NumPy also offers several functions to quickly generate arrays:

- **`np.zeros(shape)`** : Creates an array filled with zeros.

- **`np.ones(shape)`** : Creates an array filled with ones.

- **`np.arange(start, end, step)`** : Creates an array with a range of numbers.

- **`np.linspace(start, end, num)`** : Creates an array of equally spaced numbers.

Example of usage:

```
1  array_zeros = np.zeros((2, 3))
     # 2x3 matrix filled with zeros
2  array_ones = np.ones((3, 3))     # 3x3 matrix filled with ones
3  array_range = np.arange(0, 10, 2)
     # Array from 0 to 10 with step 2
4  array_linear = np.linspace(0, 1, 5)
     # Array with 5 numbers from 0 to 1
5
6  print(array_zeros)
7  print(array_ones)
8  print(array_range)
9  print(array_linear)
```

Accessing and Manipulating Arrays

Once we have created our arrays, it is important to learn how to access and manipulate their elements.

Indexing

NumPy allows access to the elements of an array using notation similar to Python lists, but with advanced features:

```python
1  # Accessing the first element of the one-dimensional array
2  print(one_dimensional_array[0])  # Output: 1
3
4
    # Accessing the element in the second row, third column of
    the matrix

5  print(two_dimensional_array[1][2])  # Output: 6
```

Slicing

Slicing in NumPy allows efficient access to sub-arrays:

```python
1
    # Getting the first three elements of the one-dimensional
    array

2  sub_array = one_dimensional_array[0:3]
    # Output: array([1, 2, 3])
3  print(sub_array)
4
5  # Getting the first row of the matrix
6  row = two_dimensional_array[0, :]  # Output: array([1, 2, 3])
7  print(row)
```

Modifying Elements

The elements of a NumPy array are mutable, which means we can change them:

```python
one_dimensional_array[0] = 10
print(one_dimensional_array)
    # Output: array([10, 2, 3, 4, 5])
```

Mathematical Operations with NumPy

One of the most important features of NumPy is the ability to perform mathematical operations on arrays efficiently.

Element-wise Operations

NumPy allows performing mathematical operations directly on arrays. For example:

```python
a = np.array([1, 2, 3])
b = np.array([4, 5, 6])

# Addition
sum_result = a + b  # Output: array([5, 7, 9])

# Subtraction
subtraction_result = b - a  # Output: array([3, 3, 3])

# Multiplication
multiplication_result = a * b  # Output: array([4, 10, 18])
```

```
12
13  # Division
14  division_result = b / a  # Output: array([4., 2.5, 2.])
```

Mathematical Functions

NumPy also includes many mathematical functions that we can apply to arrays. Here are some common examples:

```
1   array = np.array([1, 2, 3, 4, 5])
2
3   # Total sum
4   total_sum = np.sum(array)  # Output: 15
5
6   # Mean
7   mean = np.mean(array)  # Output: 3.0
8
9   # Standard deviation
10  std_deviation = np.std(array) # Output: 1.4142135623730951
11
12  # Maximum and minimum values
13  maximum = np.max(array) # Output: 5
14  minimum = np.min(array) # Output: 1
```

Matrix Operations

NumPy also allows performing operations on matrices, such as matrix multiplication:

```
1   matrix_a = np.array([[1, 2], [3, 4]])
```

```
2   matrix_b = np.array([[5, 6], [7, 8]])
3
4   # Matrix multiplication
5   matrix_product = np.dot(matrix_a, matrix_b)
        # Output: array([[19, 22], [43, 50]])
6   print(matrix_product)
```

Array Manipulation

In addition to the previous operations, NumPy provides functions to change the shape and size of arrays.

Changing the Shape of an Array

Using the reshape() method, we can change the shape of an array without changing its data:

```
1   flat_array = np.array([1, 2, 3, 4, 5, 6])
2   reshaped_array = flat_array.reshape((2, 3))
        # Changes to a 2-row and 3-column matrix
3   print(reshaped_array)  # Output: [[1 2 3], [4 5 6]]
```

Concatenating and Splitting Arrays

NumPy also provides functionalities to concatenate and split arrays:

```
1   array1 = np.array([1, 2, 3])
2   array2 = np.array([4, 5, 6])
```

```
3
4  # Concatenating arrays
5  concatenated_array = np.concatenate((array1, array2))
     # Output: array([1, 2, 3, 4, 5, 6])
6  print(concatenated_array)
7
8  # Splitting an array
9  splits = np.array_split(concatenated_array, 2)
     # Split into 2 parts
10 print(splits)  # Output: [array([1, 2, 3]), array([4, 5, 6])]
```

Conclusion

In this chapter, we explored the NumPy library and its capabilities for efficiently performing numerical computations. Learning to create and manipulate arrays, perform mathematical operations, and leverage NumPy's powerful functionality will be crucial in your journey toward mastering data science and artificial intelligence. As you progress into the following chapters, these skills will allow you to tackle more complex and in-depth tasks in data analysis. In the next chapter, we will continue our exploration with data manipulation using Pandas, a key complementary tool for any data scientist.

## Chapter 19

Data Manipulation with Pandas

Introduction

Pandas is a fundamental library in the Python ecosystem for data science. It is especially valuable for data manipulation and analysis, providing flexible and efficient data structures. With Pandas, you can perform data cleaning, transformation, and analysis tasks easily and quickly. In this chapter, we will explore the data structures offered by Pandas, particularly Series and DataFrames, and learn how to perform various data manipulation operations.

What is Pandas?

Pandas is a Python library whose name comes from the combination of

"Panel Data," a term used in econometrics that refers to data that includes multiple observations of the same object. This library is based on two main data structures:

- **Series**: Similar to a one-dimensional array or a Python list, but with labels instead of just indexes.

- **DataFrame**: A two-dimensional data structure that resembles a table or a spreadsheet, where each column can contain different types of data.

Pandas allows you to manipulate this data quickly and efficiently, opening the door to exploration and analysis of information.

Installing Pandas

To start using Pandas, we first need to install it. If you don't have it in your environment yet, you can easily do so using `pip`. Open a terminal or command prompt and run:

```
1  pip install pandas
```

Once the library is installed, you can check that the installation was successful by opening a Python console and running the following code:

```
1  import pandas as pd
2
3  print(pd.__version__)
```

This should print the installed version of Pandas, confirming that it is ready to use.

Creating Data Structures in Pandas

Series

Series is the one-dimensional data structure of Pandas. You can create a Series in various ways, but the most common is from a list:

```python
import pandas as pd

# Create a Series from a list
data = [10, 20, 30, 40, 50]
series = pd.Series(data)

print(series)
```

The output will be similar to the following:

```
0    10
1    20
2    30
3    40
4    50
dtype: int64
```

Each number in the Series has an associated index that, by default, is a set of integers starting from 0.

You can also specify your own indexes when creating a Series:

```python
# Create a Series with custom labels
data = [10, 20, 30]
labels = ['a', 'b', 'c']
```

```
4  custom_series = pd.Series(data, index=labels)
5
6  print(custom_series)
```

The output would be:

```
a    10
b    20
c    30
dtype: int64
```

DataFrames

The DataFrame is the two-dimensional data structure in Pandas, similar to a table in a database or an Excel spreadsheet. You can create a DataFrame from dictionaries, lists of lists, NumPy arrays, or CSV files.

Creating a DataFrame from a Dictionary

```
1  # Create a DataFrame from a dictionary
2  data = {
3      'Name': ['Juan', 'Ana', 'Luis'],
4      'Age': [28, 24, 30],
5      'City': ['Madrid', 'Barcelona', 'Valencia']
6  }
7  dataframe = pd.DataFrame(data)
8
9  print(dataframe)
```

This produces the following output:

```
Name   Age        City
```

```
0   Juan   28     Madrid
1    Ana   24  Barcelona
2   Luis   30   Valencia
```

Creating a DataFrame from a List of Lists

```python
1  # Create a DataFrame from a list of lists
2  data = [['Juan', 28, 'Madrid'], ['Ana', 24, 'Barcelona'], [
       'Luis', 30, 'Valencia']]
3  list_dataframe = pd.DataFrame(data, columns=['Name', 'Age',
       'City'])
4
5  print(list_dataframe)
```

The output will be the same as before, but this time created in a different way.

Accessing Data in Pandas

Once you have your DataFrame, it is vital to know how to access the data. Pandas provides several ways to access the information it contains.

Access by Columns

You can access a column of a DataFrame as if it were an attribute or using the column name as a key:

```python
1  # Access a column
2  print(dataframe['Name'])
```

```
3
4  # You can also use attribute notation
5  print(dataframe.Name)
```

Access by Rows

To access rows, you can use the `iloc[]` method, which allows access by indices, or `loc[]` used for accessing through labels:

```
1  # Access the first row
2  print(dataframe.iloc[0])  # Index
3
4  # Access a specific row by its label
5  print(dataframe.loc[0])  # Label
```

Accessing a Specific Element

To access a specific element, you can combine `iloc` and `loc` with row and column indices:

```
1  # Access a specific element
2  print(dataframe.iloc[1, 2])
     # From row 1 and column 2 -> 'Barcelona'
```

Data Manipulation

Once you have access to the data, it's time to manipulate and transform it. Here are some basic operations you can perform.

Filtering Data

Pandas makes it easy to filter data based on conditions. For example, if you want to filter people older than 25 years:

```
1  # Filter people older than 25
2  filtered = dataframe[dataframe['Age'] > 25]
3  print(filtered)
```

Modifying Data

You can modify the data in a column directly by assigning new values:

```
1  # Increase the age of each person by 1
2  dataframe['Age'] = dataframe['Age'] + 1
3  print(dataframe)
```

Adding and Removing Columns

You can also easily add or remove columns:

```
1  # Add a new column
2  dataframe['Country'] = 'Spain'
3  print(dataframe)
4
5  # Remove a column
6  dataframe.drop('Country', axis=1, inplace=True)
7  print(dataframe)
```

Grouping Data

Grouping data is a powerful feature in Pandas. It can be useful when you want to perform operations on subsets of data:

```
1  # Group by city and calculate average age
2  average_age = dataframe.groupby('City')['Age'].mean()
3  print(average_age)
```

Data Cleaning

Data cleaning is a crucial aspect of data manipulation. Pandas provides several ways to handle missing and duplicate data.

Handling Missing Values

You can identify and handle missing values in a DataFrame as follows:

```
1   # Create a DataFrame with missing values
2   nan_data = {
3       'Name': ['Juan', None, 'Luis'],
4       'Age': [28, 24, None],
5       'City': ['Madrid', 'Barcelona', None]
6   }
7   nan_dataframe = pd.DataFrame(nan_data)
8
9   # Identify missing values
10  print(nan_dataframe.isnull())
11
12  # Fill missing values
```

```
13  nan_dataframe.fillna({'Name': 'Unknown', 'Age': 0, 'City':
    'Unknown'}, inplace=True)
14  print(nan_dataframe)
15
16  # Remove rows with missing data
17  nan_dataframe.dropna(inplace=True)
18  print(nan_dataframe)
```

Detecting Duplicates

Pandas allows you to easily detect and remove duplicate rows in your DataFrame:

```
1  # Create a DataFrame with duplicates
2  duplicate_data = {
3      'Name': ['Juan', 'Ana', 'Luis', 'Juan'],
4      'Age': [28, 24, 30, 28]
5  }
6  duplicate_dataframe = pd.DataFrame(duplicate_data)
7
8  # Remove duplicate rows
9  duplicate_dataframe.drop_duplicates(inplace=True)
10  print(duplicate_dataframe)
```

Data Visualization

Although Pandas does not handle data visualization directly, it integrates easily with Matplotlib and Seaborn to create visualizations from DataFrames. Here is a basic visualization example using Matplotlib:

```
1  import matplotlib.pyplot as plt
2
3  # Plot average age by city
4  average_age.plot(kind='bar')
5  plt.title('Average Age by City')
6  plt.xlabel('City')
7  plt.ylabel('Average Age')
8  plt.show()
```

Conclusion

In this chapter, we have seen how to manipulate data using the Pandas library in Python. From creating Series and DataFrames to data manipulation and cleaning, these concepts are key to data science and working with artificial intelligence. By mastering Pandas, you will equip yourself with the tools necessary to perform deep analyses and extract valuable insights from your datasets. In the next chapter, we will delve into data visualization, a complementary skill essential in data analysis and interpretation.

## Chapter 20

Data Visualization with Matplotlib

Introduction

Data visualization is a fundamental part of data analysis, as it allows us to represent information graphically and thereby facilitate comprehension and analysis. Through graphs and diagrams, it is possible to discover patterns, identify trends, and highlight anomalies in the data that could otherwise go unnoticed in a numerical format. In this chapter, we will focus on Matplotlib, the most popular data visualization library in the Python ecosystem. We will learn how to create basic graphs, customize visualizations, and export them for use in reports and presentations.

What is Matplotlib?

Matplotlib is a plotting library in Python that provides a wide variety of tools for creating data visualizations in different formats. With Matplotlib, you can generate 2D and 3D graphs, histograms, scatter plots, heat maps, bar charts, among others. The library is highly configurable and flexible, making it a popular choice among data scientists, engineers, and analysts.

Installing Matplotlib

To start using Matplotlib, we first need to ensure that it is installed in our environment. If you don't have it yet, you can easily install it using `pip`. Open a terminal or command line and run the following command:

```
pip install matplotlib
```

Once installed, we can verify the installation by opening a Python console and running:

```
import matplotlib
print(matplotlib.__version__)
```

This should print the version of Matplotlib installed, confirming that it is ready for use.

Creating Basic Graphs

The simplest way to start visualizing with Matplotlib is by using the `pyplot` module, which provides a MATLAB-like interface. Below are several basic types of graphs you can create with this library.

Line Chart

Line charts are ideal for showing trends over time or in ordered sequences. Here's a simple example of how to create a line chart:

```python
1   import matplotlib.pyplot as plt
2
3   # Sample data
4   x = [1, 2, 3, 4, 5]
5   y = [2, 3, 5, 7, 11]
6
7   # Create a line chart
8   plt.plot(x, y)
9   plt.title('Line Chart')
10  plt.xlabel('X Axis')
11  plt.ylabel('Y Axis')
12  plt.grid()
13
14  # Show the chart
15  plt.show()
```

This code generates a line chart that represents the data contained in the lists x and y. The grid() function adds a grid to the chart, making it easier to read.

Bar Chart

Bar charts are useful for comparing different categories of data. Below is an example of how to create a bar chart:

```python
1   # Sample data
2   categories = ['A', 'B', 'C', 'D']
```

```
3   values = [3, 7, 5, 2]
4
5   # Create a bar chart
6   plt.bar(categories, values)
7   plt.title('Bar Chart')
8   plt.xlabel('Categories')
9   plt.ylabel('Values')
10  plt.grid(axis='y')
11
12  # Show the chart
13  plt.show()
```

In this example, the chart illustrates the comparison between four different categories. The `axis='y'` option in the `grid()` method only shows grid lines on the vertical axis.

Scatter Plot

Scatter plots are ideal for showing the relationship between two variables. Here's an example of how to make one:

```
1   # Sample data
2   import numpy as np
3
4   np.random.seed(0)
5   x = np.random.rand(50)   # 50 random values
6   y = np.random.rand(50)   # 50 random values
7
8   # Create a scatter plot
9   plt.scatter(x, y, color='blue', alpha=0.5)
10  plt.title('Scatter Plot')
11  plt.xlabel('X Variable')
12  plt.ylabel('Y Variable')
```

```
13
14  # Show the chart
15  plt.show()
```

In this case, `alpha` is used to adjust the transparency of the points, which can be useful when many overlapping data points are present.

Customizing Graphs

Matplotlib offers many options to customize graphs and make them more informative.

Titles and Labels

Ensuring that your graphs have clear titles and labels is crucial for facilitating understanding. As we have seen, you can add a title and labels with `title()`, `xlabel()`, and `ylabel()`.

Colors and Styles

You can change the color and style of lines, bars, and scatter points. Here's an example of how to do this in a line chart:

```
1  # Create a line chart
2  plt.plot(x, y, color='red', linestyle='--', marker='o',
      markersize=8)
3  plt.title('Customized Line Chart')
4  plt.xlabel('X Axis')
5  plt.ylabel('Y Axis')
6  plt.grid()
```

```
7
8  # Show the chart
9  plt.show()
```

In this example, the chart is customized using a red color, a dashed line style, and circular markers.

Legends

Legends are important for providing context to your graph. You can add a legend using the `legend()` method:

```
1   # Create multiple line charts
2   plt.plot(x, y, label='Series 1')
3   plt.plot(x, [i**2 for i in y], label='Series 2')
4   plt.title('Line Charts with Legend')
5   plt.xlabel('X Axis')
6   plt.ylabel('Y Axis')
7   plt.grid()
8   plt.legend()
9
10  # Show the chart
11  plt.show()
```

The `legend()` method automatically adds a legend based on the labels of the series.

Saving Charts

Once you have created and customized a chart, you may want to save it. Matplotlib makes this simple using the `savefig()` method:

```
1   # Create a bar chart
2   plt.bar(categories, values)
3   plt.title('Bar Chart')
4   plt.xlabel('Categories')
5   plt.ylabel('Values')
6   plt.grid(axis='y')
7
8   # Save the chart as a PNG file
9   plt.savefig('bar_chart.png', dpi=300)
10
11  # Show the chart
12  plt.show()
```

In this case, the chart is saved with a specific name and a resolution of 300 DPI (dots per inch), which is suitable for high-quality images.

Conclusion

Data visualization is a key component in data analysis, and Matplotlib is a powerful tool for creating effective and customizable graphs in Python. In this chapter, we covered the basics of creating simple graphs, customizing them, and how to save visualizations. As you continue your journey into the world of artificial intelligence and data science, developing skills in visualization will be essential for effectively communicating your findings. In the next chapter, we will explore advanced visualizations using Seaborn, a library built on top of Matplotlib that makes it easier to create more complex statistical graphics.

## Chapter 21

Advanced Visualization with Seaborn

Introduction

Data visualization is a fundamental aspect of data analysis that allows the transformation of numerical data sets into graphical representations. While Matplotlib is an excellent tool for creating basic and customized charts, Seaborn is built on top of Matplotlib and provides an easier and more attractive interface for creating complex and statistically informative visualizations.

Seaborn is specifically designed to work with statistical data and makes data visualization more intuitive and accessible. In this chapter, we will explore the features and capabilities of Seaborn, learn how to integrate this library with pandas, and how to create more advanced visualizations that enhance data exploration and understanding.

What is Seaborn?

Seaborn is a data visualization library based on Matplotlib. Its focus is on simplicity and ease of use, making it a popular choice among data scientists. Seaborn provides a richer set of visualizations and aesthetically pleasing designs that allow exploration of patterns and relationships in complex data, as well as the inclusion of statistical elements such as confidence intervals and regression fits.

Installing Seaborn

To use Seaborn, it must first be installed. You can do this using the package manager `pip`. Run the following command in your terminal or command line:

```
1  pip install seaborn
```

Once installed, verify the installation by opening a Python console and running:

```
1  import seaborn as sns
2  print(sns.__version__)
```

This should display the installed version of Seaborn, confirming that it is ready for use.

Integration with Pandas

Seaborn is designed to work effectively with pandas DataFrames. This means you can use your existing pandas datasets without needing to transform them. The integration between both libraries allows for simpler and more natural visualizations.

Loading Data

To illustrate how to use Seaborn, we first need a dataset. Seaborn includes several example datasets that you can use for practice. One of the most well-known is the "tips" dataset, which contains information about tips in a restaurant.

To load it, you can use the following code:

```
1  import seaborn as sns
2
3  # Load the example dataset "tips"
4  tips = sns.load_dataset('tips')
5  print(tips.head())
```

This code will load the "tips" dataset and display the first five rows. This will allow you to see the structure of the DataFrame, which includes columns such as `total_bill`, `tip`, `sex`, `smoker`, `day`, `time`, and `size`.

Creating Charts with Seaborn

Next, we'll look at some of the most common visualizations you can create using Seaborn.

Scatter Plot

A scatter plot is useful for visualizing the relationship between two variables. We can use the `scatterplot()` method from Seaborn to create one.

```
1  import matplotlib.pyplot as plt
2
3  # Create a scatter plot
4  sns.scatterplot(data=tips, x='total_bill', y='tip', hue=
     'time', style='sex')
5  plt.title('Scatter Plot of Total Bill vs Tip')
6  plt.xlabel('Total Bill ($)')
7  plt.ylabel('Tip ($)')
8  plt.show()
```

In this plot, we use `hue` to add an additional dimension to the graph, displaying time (lunch or dinner) and `style` to differentiate between men and women. The visual representation quickly allows the viewer to analyze the relationship between the bill amount and the tip.

Bar Plot

Bar plots are ideal for comparing proportions of different categories. Seaborn offers the `barplot()` method, which allows representing the mean of a categorical variable compared to another.

```
1  # Average tips by day
2  sns.barplot(data=tips, x='day', y='tip', hue='sex')
3  plt.title('Average Tips by Day and Gender')
4  plt.ylabel('Average Tip ($)')
5  plt.xlabel('Day of the Week')
6  plt.show()
```

In this example, we compare the mean tips by day, differentiated by gender. This clearly shows how tips vary by day of the week and the gender of the person paying the bill.

Box Plot

The box plot is a powerful tool for showing the distribution and variability of data. This type of plot allows for the identification of outliers and comparisons across categories.

```
1  # Create a box plot
2  sns.boxplot(data=tips, x='day', y='total_bill', hue='smoker',
     palette='muted')
3  plt.title(
     'Distribution of Total Bill by Day and Smoking Status')
4  plt.ylabel('Total Bill ($)')
5  plt.xlabel('Day of the Week')
6  plt.show()
```

In this plot, the variable `smoker` is used as an additional category, allowing us to observe the differences in total bills between smoking and non-smoking customers throughout the week.

Pairplot

The `pairplot` is one of the most useful visualizations in Seaborn, as it allows seeing the relationships among all numerical variables in a DataFrame, presenting scatter plots for each combination of variables and density plots along the diagonal.

```
1  # Create a pairplot of the data
2  sns.pairplot(tips, hue='sex')
3  plt.title('Relationships among Variables in the Tips Dataset'
     )
4  plt.show()
```

The `pairplot` allows for observing interactions between different variables, which is useful for quickly gaining an overview of the relationships in the data.

Heatmap

Heatmaps are useful for visualizing the correlation matrix among various numerical variables. Seaborn offers `heatmap`, which allows you to represent this matrix visually.

```python
1  # Calculate the correlation matrix
2  corr = tips.corr()
3
4  # Create a heatmap
5  sns.heatmap(corr, annot=True, cmap='coolwarm')
6  plt.title('Correlation Matrix')
7  plt.show()
```

In this example, the `heatmap` displays the correlations between all numerical variables in the dataset, with annotations indicating the correlation coefficients. This helps you quickly understand which variables are related to one another.

Customizing Charts

Like Matplotlib, Seaborn allows customizing charts in several ways:

- **Colors**: You can specify color palettes using the `palette` argument in Seaborn functions. For example, `palette='bright'`, `palette='pastel'`, etc., allow for different visual styles.

- **Style Adjustments**: Seaborn allows changing the style of plots through `sns.set_style()`. You can choose from styles such as "darkgrid", "whitegrid", "dark", "white", and "ticks".

```
1  sns.set_style('whitegrid')  # Change background style
```

- **Titles and Labels**: Just like with Matplotlib, you can add titles and axis labels using the `title()`, `xlabel()`, and `ylabel()` functions.

Conclusion

In this chapter, we explored how to use Seaborn to create advanced and more informative visualizations that complement our graphical representations. From scatter plots to box plots and pairplots, Seaborn makes it easy to visualize patterns and relationships in complex datasets.

As you continue your journey in the world of artificial intelligence and data science, mastering advanced visualization with Seaborn will be essential for effectively communicating your findings and better understanding the data you are analyzing. Visualization is a powerful tool for data interpretation, and with the combination of pandas and Seaborn, you will be well-equipped to tackle more complex data analysis problems in the future.

## Chapter 22

Fundamental Concepts of Statistics

Introduction

Statistics is a discipline that provides tools and methods for collecting, analyzing, and interpreting data. In the context of artificial intelligence (AI) and data science, statistics plays a fundamental role, as it allows us to extract valuable information from data and make evidence-based decisions. In this chapter, we will address the basic concepts of statistics that will help establish a solid understanding for the subsequent use of more advanced techniques in AI models.

Measures of Central Tendency

Measures of central tendency are values that describe a dataset by identifying the central point within a set of values. The three most common measures are the mean, the median, and the mode.

Mean

The arithmetic mean, commonly known as the average, is calculated by summing all the values and dividing the result by the total number of values. For example, if we have a dataset that represents the ages of a group of people:

```
1  ages = [22, 25, 29, 35, 29]
2  mean = sum(ages) / len(ages)
3  print("The mean of ages is:", mean)  # Output: 26.0
```

In this case, the mean age is 26.0. The mean is a good indicator of central tendency but can be influenced by outliers. For example, if we add an extremely high age:

```
1  ages.append(100)  # Adding another age
2  atypical_mean = sum(ages) / len(ages)
3  print("The new mean of ages is:", atypical_mean)
      # Output: 29.0
```

The new mean changes significantly due to the outlier.

Median

The median is the value that divides an ordered dataset into two equal parts. To calculate it, we first sort the dataset and then find the middle value. If the number of observations is odd, the median is the central value. If it is even, the median is the average of the two central numbers.

```
1   import numpy as np
2
3   sorted_ages = sorted(ages)
4   n = len(sorted_ages)
5
6   if n % 2 == 0:
7       # If there is an even number of observations
8       median = (sorted_ages[n//2 - 1] + sorted_ages[n//2]) / 2
9   else:
10      # If there is an odd number of observations
11      median = sorted_ages[n//2]
12
13  print("The median of ages is:", median)
```

The median is particularly useful in datasets with outliers, as it is not affected in the same way as the mean.

Mode

The mode is the value that appears most frequently in a dataset. There can be multiple modes in a dataset if several values are equally present.

```
1   from scipy import stats
2
3   mode = stats.mode(ages).mode[0]
4   print("The mode of ages is:", mode)   # Output: 29
```

In this example, the mode of the ages is 29, as it is the number that appears most frequently in the dataset.

Measures of Dispersion

Measures of dispersion indicate the degree of variability or diversity in a dataset. The main measures of dispersion are the range, variance, and standard deviation.

Range

The range is the difference between the maximum value and the minimum value of a dataset. It is a simple calculation that provides a basic idea of dispersion:

```
1  range_value = max(ages) - min(ages)
2  print("The range of ages is:", range_value)  # Output: 78
```

Although the range is useful, it does not capture all the variability of the data.

Variance

Variance measures the average of the squared differences from the mean. The greater the variance, the greater the dispersion of the dataset.

```
1  variance = sum((x - mean) ** 2 for x in ages) / (len(ages) -
   1)
2  print("The variance of ages is:", variance)
```

Standard Deviation

The standard deviation is the square root of the variance and provides a measure of dispersion in the same units as the original data. It is one of the most widely used measures to determine variability.

```
1  standard_deviation = variance ** 0.5
2  print("The standard deviation of ages is:",
       standard_deviation)
```

Both measures, variance and standard deviation, help us understand how dispersed our data is concerning the mean.

Graphical Representation of Data

Graphical representation is a crucial part of statistical analysis as it allows us to visualize patterns and relationships in data. There are several ways to graphically represent data, including histograms, boxplots, and scatter plots.

Histograms

A histogram is a graphical representation that shows the distribution of a set of values by grouping them into intervals (or bins). It helps visualize the shape of the distribution of the data.

```
1  import matplotlib.pyplot as plt
2
3  plt.hist(ages, bins=5, alpha=0.7, color='blue')
4  plt.title('Histogram of Ages')
5  plt.xlabel('Age')
6  plt.ylabel('Frequency')
7  plt.grid()
8  plt.show()
```

In this histogram, we can observe how the ages are distributed across different intervals, which can help identify patterns in the data.

Boxplots

Boxplots show the median, quartiles, and outliers, providing a compact view of the data's distribution.

```
1  plt.boxplot(ages)
2  plt.title('Boxplot of Ages')
3  plt.ylabel('Age')
4  plt.grid()
5  plt.show()
```

This graph is very useful for detecting the presence of outliers and observing the dispersion of the data.

Conclusion

In this chapter, we have covered the fundamental concepts of statistics, including measures of central tendency and dispersion, as well as the graphical representation of data. These concepts are essential for any data scientist and researcher in the field of artificial intelligence, as they will serve as a foundation for deeper and more advanced analyses in subsequent chapters. Having a solid understanding of statistics will enable you to effectively interpret data and make informed decisions based on it.

## Chapter 23

Probabilities and Distributions

Introduction

Probability is a branch of mathematics that studies uncertainty and describes the likelihood of an event occurring. In the context of artificial intelligence and machine learning, understanding probability is fundamental, as many models and algorithms are based on probabilistic principles to make inferences and decisions.

In this chapter, we will explore the basic concepts of probability and some of the most common probability distributions. Through examples, we will learn to apply these concepts to real-world problems, which will serve as a foundation for understanding AI algorithms that utilize statistics and inference.

Basic Concepts of Probability

The probability of an event is a number between 0 and 1 that indicates how likely it is that the event will occur. A probability of 0 means that the event will not occur, while a probability of 1 means that the event will certainly occur.

Sample Space

The sample space is the set of all possible outcomes of a random experiment. For example, if we roll a die, the sample space is:

```
S = {1, 2, 3, 4, 5, 6}
```

Each outcome in the sample space has an equal probability of occurring, which is $\frac{1}{6}$ for a fair die.

Events

An event is a subset of the sample space. For example, if we want to know the probability of rolling an even number on a die, the event would be:

```
E = {2, 4, 6}
```

The probability of this event occurring is:

$$P(E) = \frac{\text{number of favorable outcomes}}{\text{total number of outcomes}} = \frac{3}{6} = \frac{1}{2}$$

Independent and Dependent Events

There are two main types of events considered in probability:

1. **Independent Events**: Two events are independent if the occurrence of one does not affect the occurrence of the other. For example, rolling a die and flipping a coin are independent events.

2. **Dependent Events**: If the occurrence of one event affects the probability of another occurring, they are considered dependent events. For example, drawing cards from a deck without replacement is an example of dependent events, as the composition of the deck changes after each draw.

Bayes' Theorem

Bayes' theorem is one of the foundations of probability and allows us to update the probability of an event as new information becomes available. The theorem is given by the formula:

$$P(A \mid B) = \frac{P(B \mid A) \cdot P(A)}{P(B)}$$

Where:

- $P(A \mid B)$ is the probability of event A occurring given that event B has occurred.

- $P(B \mid A)$ is the probability of event B occurring given that event A has occurred.

- $P(A)$ and $P(B)$ are the prior probabilities of events A and B, respectively.

Example of Bayes' Theorem

Suppose there is a disease that affects 1% of the population. A test is conducted that gives a positive result with a 90% accuracy if the person is sick and has a 5% false positive rate for healthy individuals. We want to know the probability that a person is actually sick given that they tested positive.

We define the events:

- A: The person is sick.

- B: The test result is positive.

The known values are:

- $P(A) = 0.01$

- $P(B \mid A) = 0.9$

- $P(B \mid A') = 0.05$ (where A' is the event that the person is not sick)

Now we calculate $P(B)$: $P(B) = P(B \mid A) \cdot P(A) + P(B \mid A') \cdot P(A') = (0.9 \cdot 0.01) + (0.05 \cdot 0.99) = 0.009 + 0.0495 = 0.0585$

Then, using Bayes' theorem: $P(A \mid B) = \frac{P(B \mid A) \cdot P(A)}{P(B)} = \frac{0.9 \cdot 0.01}{0.0585} \approx 0.1538$

That is, there is approximately a 15.38% probability that the person is actually sick, even though the test was positive.

Probability Distributions

Probability distributions describe how probabilities are distributed over a set of possible outcomes. The two main categories of distributions are:

1. **Discrete Distributions**: These are used to model situations where outcomes are finite or countable. A common example is the Poisson distribution.

2. **Continuous Distributions**: These are used to model situations where outcomes are infinite and cannot be counted discretely. A

common example is the normal distribution.

Binomial Distribution

The binomial distribution is used to model the number of successes in a fixed number of independent trials, each with the same probability of success. The formula for calculating the probability of obtaining exactly k successes in n trials is:

$$P(X = k) = \binom{n}{k}p^k(1-p)^{n-k}$$

Where:

- n is the number of trials.

- k is the number of desired successes.

- p is the probability of success in a single trial.

- $\binom{n}{k}$ is the binomial coefficient.

Example of Binomial Distribution

Imagine we flip a fair coin 10 times, and we want to calculate the probability of getting exactly 6 heads. Here, $n = 10$, $k = 6$, and $p = 0.5$.

Using the binomial distribution formula:

```
from scipy.stats import binom

# Define the parameters
n = 10  # number of flips
k = 6   # number of desired heads
p = 0.5 # probability of heads
```

```
7
8   # Calculate the probability
9   probability = binom.pmf(k, n, p)
10  print(f"The probability of getting exactly {k} heads in {n}
        flips is: {probability:.4f}")
```

Normal Distribution

The normal distribution, also known as the Gaussian distribution, is one of the most important probability distributions in statistics. It is characterized by its bell-shaped curve and is defined by two parameters: the mean (μ) and the standard deviation (σ).

The probability density function of the normal distribution is given by:

$$f(x) = \frac{1}{\sigma\sqrt{2\pi}} e^{-\frac{(x-\mu)^2}{2\sigma^2}}$$

Example of Normal Distribution

Suppose the heights of a group of people are approximately normal, with a mean of 170 cm and a standard deviation of 10 cm. We can use the normal distribution to calculate the probability that a randomly chosen person has a height greater than 180 cm.

```
1   from scipy.stats import norm
2
3   # Define the parameters
4   mu = 170  # mean
5   sigma = 10 # standard deviation
6
7   # Calculate the probability of being greater than 180 cm
```

```
8  probability = 1 - norm.cdf(180, mu, sigma)
9  print(
     f"The probability that a person is taller than 180 cm is: {
     probability:.4f}")
```

Conclusion

In this chapter, we explored the basic concepts of probability, including its definition, sample space, events, and Bayes' theorem. We also analyzed the most relevant probability distributions, such as the binomial distribution and the normal distribution. These concepts are fundamental to understanding how many machine learning and statistical algorithms work. As you continue your study of artificial intelligence, these fundamentals will help you build more robust models and interpret data meaningfully.

## Chapter 24

Statistical Inference

Introduction

Statistical inference is a branch of statistics that deals with making generalizations about a population from a sample. As we collect data and analyze it, it is natural to want to make claims about a larger group. However, when working with only a sample of data, we must be cautious and apply appropriate techniques to ensure that our conclusions are valid and accurate. This chapter will focus on the concepts of estimation and hypothesis testing, which are two fundamental tools of statistical inference.

Estimation

Estimation is the process by which we use information from a sample to infer characteristics about a population. There are two types of estimators:

Point Estimators

Point estimators are single values used to approximate a population parameter. For example, the sample mean is used to estimate the population mean. If we have a sample of data, we can calculate its mean as follows:

```python
import numpy as np

# Suppose we have a sample of heights in centimeters
sample_heights = [165, 170, 175, 160, 180]

# Calculate the sample mean
sample_mean = np.mean(sample_heights)
print(f"The sample mean of the heights is: {sample_mean:.2f} cm")
```

In this example, the sample mean would be a point estimator of the population mean of all heights in a larger group.

Interval Estimators

Unlike point estimators, confidence intervals provide a range within which the true population parameter is expected to lie. A 95% confidence interval indicates that if multiple samples were taken and confidence intervals were calculated for each, approximately 95% of those intervals would include the true population parameter.

Calculating the Confidence Interval

To calculate a confidence interval for the population mean with a 95%

confidence level, we use the formula:

$$CI = \bar{x} \pm z\left(\frac{s}{\sqrt{n}}\right)$$

Where:

- $\bar{x}$ is the sample mean.

- z is the critical value from the normal distribution (for 95% confidence, $z \approx 1.96$).

- s is the sample standard deviation.

- n is the sample size.

Let's look at an example of this calculation:

```python
import scipy.stats as stats

# Sample data
n = len(sample_heights)
sample_mean = np.mean(sample_heights)
sample_std_dev = np.std(sample_heights, ddof=1)

# Critical value for a 95% confidence interval
z = stats.norm.ppf(0.975)
    # 0.975 because we want the area to the left of z

# Calculate the margin of error
margin_of_error = z * (sample_std_dev / np.sqrt(n))

# Calculate the confidence interval
confidence_interval = (sample_mean - margin_of_error,
    sample_mean + margin_of_error)

print(f"The 95% confidence interval is: {confidence_interval[
    0]:.2f} cm - {confidence_interval[1]:.2f} cm")
```

These calculations allow us to infer with a specific level of confidence that the population mean lies within the determined interval.

Hypothesis Testing

Once we understand how to make estimates of population parameters, the next step is to conduct hypothesis tests. A hypothesis is a statement about a population parameter that we want to test. In hypothesis testing, we formulate two statements:

- **Null Hypothesis (H_0)**: This is the initial statement that generally suggests there is no effect or difference.

- **Alternative Hypothesis (H_1)**: This is the statement we want to prove, which contradicts the null hypothesis.

Steps in Hypothesis Testing

The general steps we follow in a hypothesis test include:

1. **Formulate the Hypotheses**: Define H_0 and H_1.

2. **Select a Significance Level**: Commonly, an alpha (α) of 0.05 is used.

3. **Choose the Appropriate Statistical Test**: Depending on the type of data and the nature of the hypothesis.

4. **Calculate the Test Statistic**: Use our data to obtain a statistic.

5. **Make a Decision**: Compare the test statistic with a critical value or calculate a p-value.

Example of Hypothesis Testing

Suppose we are interested in knowing whether the mean of a population is equal to 170 cm ($H_0 : \mu = 170$). We will use a t-test for a single sample if we have a small sample size and do not know the population standard deviation.

Calculating the t Statistic

The t statistic is calculated as follows:

$$t = \frac{\bar{x} - \mu_0}{\frac{s}{\sqrt{n}}}$$

Where:

- $\bar{x}$ is the sample mean.

- μ_0 is the value under the null hypothesis.

- s is the sample standard deviation.

- n is the sample size.

Let's see how to carry this out in Python:

```python
# Null hypothesis
mu_0 = 170  # population mean under H0

# Calculate t statistic
t_statistic = (sample_mean - mu_0) / (sample_std_dev / np.sqrt(n))
print(f"The t statistic is: {t_statistic:.4f}")
```

Comparing with Critical Values

Now, we need to determine the critical values to decide whether to reject the null hypothesis. For this, we use the Student's t distribution and the significance level (α).

```
1  # Determine the critical value
2  degrees_of_freedom = n - 1
3  critical_value = stats.t.ppf(1 - 0.05, degrees_of_freedom)
4  print(
       f"The critical value for a significance level of 0.05 is: {
       critical_value:.4f}")
```

If the calculated t statistic is greater than the critical value, we reject H_0, suggesting that there is sufficient evidence to accept H_1.

Interpreting Results

Once we have compared the t statistic with the critical value:

- If $|t|$ > critical value: We reject H_0.

- If $|t|$ ≤ critical value: There is not enough evidence to reject H_0.

We can also choose to calculate the p-value, which represents the probability of obtaining results at least as extreme as those observed, given that the null hypothesis is true.

```
1  # Calculate the p-value
2  p_value = 2 * (1 - stats.t.cdf(abs(t_statistic),
       degrees_of_freedom))
```

```
3  print(f"The p-value is: {p_value:.4f}")
```

The final decision will depend on comparing the p-value with the significance level.

Conclusion

Statistical inference is an essential component in data science and artificial intelligence, as it allows us to make claims about populations based on sample data. We have explored two key tools: estimation and hypothesis testing. Through practical examples in Python, we have seen how to calculate confidence intervals, perform hypothesis tests, and make data-driven decisions. Mastering these concepts is fundamental to conducting meaningful analyses and making reliable predictions in the field of AI and beyond.

## Chapter 25

Data Cleaning and Preprocessing

Introduction

In data analysis, cleaning and preprocessing are crucial steps before applying any artificial intelligence or machine learning model. Raw data often contain errors, missing values, duplicates, and noise, which can lead to misleading or inaccurate results. In this chapter, we will explore various techniques for cleaning and preprocessing data using Python, which will help improve the quality of our analyses and maximize the effectiveness of our AI models.

Importance of Data Cleaning

The quality of the data directly impacts the quality of the decisions we make based on that data. A clean and well-structured dataset can lead to more accurate models, while unwanted data can result in misinterpretations and biased outcomes. Data cleaning involves identifying and correcting errors as well as ensuring the data is consistent and in a suitable format for analysis.

Effects of Dirty Data on Analysis

Here are some negative effects of working with unclean data:

- **Missing Values**: They can bias results or lead to errors in analysis.

- **Duplicates**: They can cause artificial inflation of certain metrics (e.g., averages) and distort reality.

- **Inconsistencies**: Differences in the way data is entered (e.g., 'Yes', 'yes', and 'YES') can lead to confusion and incorrect results.

- **Noise**: Irrelevant or erroneous data can disrupt the analytical process and reduce the model's accuracy.

Handling Missing Values

Missing values are a common problem in data cleaning. If not handled properly, they can lead to biases in the model and affect learning. Below, we will discuss several strategies to address missing values.

Identifying Missing Values

To identify missing values in a pandas DataFrame, you can use the `isnull()` method combined with `sum()` to count how many values are missing in each column:

```
1  import pandas as pd
2
3  # Load example data
4  data = {'Name': ['Alice', 'Bob', 'Charlie', None],
5          'Age': [25, None, 30, 22],
6          'City': ['New York', 'Los Angeles', None, 'Chicago']}
7
8  df = pd.DataFrame(data)
9
10 # Count missing values
11 missing_values = df.isnull().sum()
12 print(missing_values)
```

This will print the number of missing values in each column of the DataFrame.

Strategies for Handling Missing Values

There are different approaches to handle missing values:

1. **Removing Rows or Columns**: If there are too many missing values in a row or column, it may be better to remove it.

   ```
   1  # Remove rows with missing values
   2  df_without_missing = df.dropna()
   ```

2. **Imputation**: Missing values can be filled with the mean, median, or mode of the column. This is a common technique to preserve information.

   ```
   1  # Impute the mean in the 'Age' column
   2  df['Age'].fillna(df['Age'].mean(), inplace=True)
   ```

3. **Using a Predictive Model**: For missing values in critical columns, a model can be trained to predict the missing values based on other features.

4. **Default Values**: If it makes sense to do so, default values can be used to fill in missing values.

Detecting and Removing Duplicates

Duplicates can distort the representation of the data. To detect duplicates in a DataFrame, you can use the duplicated() method:

```
1  # Detect duplicates
2  duplicates = df.duplicated()
3  print(df[duplicates])
```

To remove duplicates, the drop_duplicates() method is used:

```
1  # Remove duplicates
2  unique_df = df.drop_duplicates()
```

This ensures that each record in your dataset is unique and representative.

Normalization and Standardization of Data

Normalization and standardization are techniques used to adjust the scale of the data, ensuring that no features dominate others due to their range of values.

Normalization

Normalization reshapes features to a specific range, typically between 0 and 1. This can be done using Min-Max Scaling:

```
1  from sklearn.preprocessing import MinMaxScaler
2
3  scaler = MinMaxScaler()
4  df[['Age']] = scaler.fit_transform(df[['Age']])
```

Standardization

Standardization involves adjusting the data so that it has a mean of 0 and a standard deviation of 1, using the following formula:

$$z = \frac{x - \mu}{\sigma}$$

```
1  from sklearn.preprocessing import StandardScaler
2
3  scaler = StandardScaler()
4  df[['Age']] = scaler.fit_transform(df[['Age']])
```

The choice between normalization and standardization depends on the nature of the data and the AI algorithm that is planned to be used.

Encoding Categorical Variables

Categorical variables need to be converted into a numerical format to be utilized in machine learning algorithms. Several encoding techniques are prominent:

One-Hot Encoding

One-hot encoding creates binary columns for each possible category. For example, if a column `City` has three categories, three binary columns will be created.

```
1   df_encoded = pd.get_dummies(df, columns=['City'], drop_first=
    True)
```

Label Encoding

Label encoding assigns an integer to each category but is more suitable only for ordinal variables.

```
1   from sklearn.preprocessing import LabelEncoder
2
3   encoder = LabelEncoder()
4   df['City'] = encoder.fit_transform(df['City'])
```

Both techniques are useful, but the choice of which to apply depends on the specific algorithm that will be used.

Transformations and Final Cleaning

Once you have handled missing values, removed duplicates, and encoded categorical variables, the next step is to perform some additional transformations and final adjustments.

Handling Outliers

Outliers are observations that deviate significantly from other data. It is important to identify them and decide whether they should be removed or adjusted. To detect them, methods like the interquartile range (IQR) can be used:

```
1  Q1 = df['Age'].quantile(0.25)
2  Q3 = df['Age'].quantile(0.75)
3  IQR = Q3 - Q1
4
5  # Filter out outliers
6  df_without_outliers = df[(df['Age'] >= (Q1 - 1.5 * IQR)) & (
       df['Age'] <= (Q3 + 1.5 * IQR))]
```

Data Formatting

Ensure that the columns are in the correct data type. For example, numbers should be of numeric data types and categories should be strings or specific categories.

```
1  df['Name'] = df['Name'].astype(str)
2  df['Age'] = df['Age'].astype(float)
```

Conclusion

Data cleaning and preprocessing is an essential step in data analysis and in developing artificial intelligence models. By identifying and managing missing values, duplicates, and normalizing or standardizing variables, we can significantly improve the quality of our data. Additionally, proper encoding of categorical variables and handling outliers will allow our models to be more accurate and reliable. By mastering these techniques, the reader will be better prepared to tackle data analysis and artificial intelligence model projects with confidence.

## Chapter 26

Data Transformation Techniques

Introduction

Data preprocessing is a crucial stage in the data analysis lifecycle and artificial intelligence model development. One of the most important aspects of preprocessing is data transformation, which involves modifying raw data to make it suitable for analysis and modeling. In this chapter, we will explore various data transformation techniques, including normalization, standardization, categorical variable encoding, and dimensionality reduction. These techniques will help us obtain a cleaner and more effective dataset that facilitates the performance of AI models.

Normalization and Standardization

Normalization

Normalization is the process of scaling data to a specific range, typically between 0 and 1. This is especially important in machine learning algorithms that use distance, such as K-nearest neighbors (KNN) and logistic regression, as the scale of features can influence the calculated distance between data points.

Normalization Example:

Suppose we have a dataset that includes the height and weight of different individuals:

```python
1  import pandas as pd
2
3  data = {
4      'Height': [160, 165, 170, 175, 180],
5      'Weight': [60, 65, 70, 75, 80]
6  }
7
8  df = pd.DataFrame(data)
```

To normalize these data between 0 and 1, we use the Min-Max scaling formula:

$$X_{norm} = \frac{X - X_{min}}{X_{max} - X_{min}}$$

Next, we apply this transformation using the MinMaxScaler from the sklearn library:

```
1  from sklearn.preprocessing import MinMaxScaler
2
3  scaler = MinMaxScaler()
4  df_normalized = pd.DataFrame(scaler.fit_transform(df),
       columns=df.columns)
5  print(df_normalized)
```

The result will be a DataFrame where all heights and weights are scaled to a range of 0 to 1.

Standardization

Standardization, on the other hand, refers to the transformation of data so that it has a mean of 0 and a standard deviation of 1. It is useful when data has different scales, and we need the features to be comparable.

The formula for standardization is:

$$X_{std} = \frac{X - \mu}{\sigma}$$

Where μ is the mean and σ is the standard deviation.

Standardization Example:

Let's take the same dataset and standardize the heights and weights:

```
1  from sklearn.preprocessing import StandardScaler
2
3  scaler = StandardScaler()
4  df_standardized = pd.DataFrame(scaler.fit_transform(df),
       columns=df.columns)
5  print(df_standardized)
```

In this case, the height and weight columns will have a mean of 0 and a standard deviation of 1, allowing for fair comparison between them.

Categorical Variable Encoding

Categorical variables are those that represent discrete categories, and many AI algorithms require data to be numeric. Therefore, it is necessary to transform these variables into a numeric format.

One-Hot Encoding

One-hot encoding transforms each category into a new binary column. For example, if a categorical variable has three different categories, three columns will be created, each representing a category.

One-Hot Encoding Example:

Imagine a dataset that has a column for colors:

```
1  data = {
2      'Color': ['Red', 'Green', 'Blue', 'Green', 'Red']
3  }
4
5  df_colors = pd.DataFrame(data)
```

We can apply one-hot encoding as follows:

```
1  df_encoded = pd.get_dummies(df_colors, columns=['Color'],
       prefix='', prefix_sep='')
2  print(df_encoded)
```

The result will be a DataFrame where each color has been transformed into binary columns: one column for Red, another for Green, and another for

Blue.

Label Encoding

Label encoding converts categorical variables into integer numbers. This technique is suitable for ordinal variables where there is a natural order among categories.

Label Encoding Example:

If we have a variable Rating with values 'Low', 'Medium', and 'High', we can assign them the numbers 1, 2, and 3 respectively:

```python
data = {
    'Rating': ['Low', 'High', 'Medium', 'Medium', 'Low']
}

df_ratings = pd.DataFrame(data)

from sklearn.preprocessing import LabelEncoder

encoder = LabelEncoder()
df_ratings['Rating'] = encoder.fit_transform(df_ratings[
    'Rating'])
print(df_ratings)
```

This transforms the Rating variable into integers, making it easier to use in numerical models.

Data Transformations

Distribution Normalization

Sometimes, data does not follow a normal distribution, which can affect the performance of certain models. Applying transformations such as the logarithm or square root can help normalize the distribution.

Logarithmic Normalization Example:

If we have a variable that has a skewed distribution:

```python
import numpy as np

data = {
    'Income': [1000, 1500, 3000, 7000, 20000]
}

df_income = pd.DataFrame(data)
df_income['Income_Log'] = np.log1p(df_income['Income'])
    # log1p is log(1+x)
print(df_income)
```

This transformation reduces the skew and helps models learn better.

Dimensionality Reduction

Dimensionality reduction is a crucial technique in data preprocessing, especially when working with datasets with many features. Techniques such as PCA (Principal Component Analysis) can help reduce the number of features while retaining most of the variability in the data.

PCA Example:

Imagine we have a dataset with many dimensions. We can use PCA to reduce it to the two most significant dimensions.

```python
from sklearn.decomposition import PCA

df_matrix = pd.DataFrame({
    'X1': [1, 2, 3, 4, 5],
    'X2': [5, 4, 3, 2, 1],
    'X3': [2, 2, 3, 4, 5]
})

pca = PCA(n_components=2)
pca_results = pca.fit_transform(df_matrix)

print(pca_results)
```

This approach helps simplify the data and focus on the most influential features, which can improve model performance.

Conclusion

Data transformation techniques are essential for preparing a dataset for analysis and modeling. Throughout this chapter, we have reviewed various techniques, such as normalization and standardization, categorical variable encoding, as well as specific transformations like logarithmic normalization and dimensionality reduction. Understanding and correctly applying these techniques can make a significant difference in the quality of the data we use, which in turn directly impacts the performance of artificial intelligence models. By the end of this chapter, the reader should feel equipped to implement these techniques in their own data analysis and modeling projects with confidence.

## Chapter 27

Creating Effective Visualizations

Introduction

Data visualization is a powerful tool in data analysis and the field of artificial intelligence. An effective visualization can provide clear insights, highlight important patterns, and help communicate conclusions in an understandable way. However, not all visualizations are created equal; some can be confusing or misleading if not designed properly. In this chapter, we will explore design principles for creating effective visualizations, types of graphs, and best practices for communicating data clearly and accurately.

Design Principles for Visualizations

Creating effective visualizations is not just about selecting an appropriate graph, but also about how the data is presented. Below are several design principles that every visualizer should consider:

Clarity

Clarity means that the visualization should be easy to understand. This includes the use of clear labels, a comprehensible legend, and the choice of colors that aid, not confuse. Avoid using unnecessarily complex graphs.

Example:

A bar chart showing the number of students in different university majors should have well-labeled axes and a legend, if necessary.

Accuracy

It is essential that the data is represented accurately. Ensure that the scales are appropriate and do not distort the information.

Example:

If a pie chart shows proportions, make sure that the size of each slice corresponds to the actual proportion of the category relative to the total.

Context

Providing context is key for the viewer to understand the visualization. This may include annotations, descriptions, or any additional information that helps interpret the data.

Example:

When presenting a line graph that shows the evolution of global temperatures, adding annotations about significant climate events will provide useful context for interpretation.

Simplicity

Sometimes, less is more. Do not overload your visualizations with unnecessary information or aesthetic elements that do not contribute to the understanding of the data.

Example:

If you are representing data in a bar chart, avoid using unnecessary backgrounds or images that distract from the main message.

Types of Graphs and When to Use Them

Selecting the right type of graph is essential to represent your data in the best possible way. Here are some of the most common types of graphs and their recommended uses:

Bar Chart

Bar charts are ideal for comparing categorical values. Each bar represents a category, and its length is proportional to its value.

```
1  import pandas as pd
2  import matplotlib.pyplot as plt
```

```
3
4    data = {'Major': ['Engineering', 'Medicine', 'Arts',
        'Sciences'],
5            'Students': [150, 200, 75, 120]}
6    df = pd.DataFrame(data)
7
8    plt.bar(df['Major'], df['Students'], color='skyblue')
9    plt.title('Number of Students by Major')
10   plt.xlabel('Major')
11   plt.ylabel('Number of Students')
12   plt.show()
```

Line Chart

A line chart is useful for showing trends over time. It connects data points with lines, allowing observation of changes and patterns.

```
1    import numpy as np
2
3    years = np.arange(2015, 2021)
4    sales = [200, 250, 300, 350, 450, 500]
5
6    plt.plot(years, sales, marker='o', color='green')
7    plt.title('Annual Sales of a Product')
8    plt.xlabel('Year')
9    plt.ylabel('Sales (in thousands)')
10   plt.xticks(years)  # To show all x-axis labels
11   plt.grid()
12   plt.show()
```

Scatter Plot

Scatter plots show the relationship between two numerical variables. Each point on the chart represents a pair of values.

```
1  x = np.random.rand(50)
2  y = np.random.rand(50)
3
4  plt.scatter(x, y, color='orange', alpha=0.7)
5  plt.title('Scatter Plot of Random Variables')
6  plt.xlabel('Variable X')
7  plt.ylabel('Variable Y')
8  plt.show()
```

Pie Chart

Pie charts are useful for showing proportions of a total. While they can be visually appealing, they should be used with caution, as they can be hard to interpret.

```
1  sizes = [15, 30, 45, 10]
2  labels = ['A', 'B', 'C', 'D']
3
4  plt.pie(sizes, labels=labels, autopct='%1.1f%%', startangle=
     140)
5  plt.title('Category Distribution')
6  plt.axis('equal')  # To make the circle
7  plt.show()
```

Integrating Multiple Graphs

In some cases, it is beneficial to combine several graphs into a single visualization to provide a more complete picture. This can be achieved through subplots in one figure.

```python
1  fig, axs = plt.subplots(2, 1, figsize=(8, 10))
2
3  # Bar chart
4  axs[0].bar(df['Major'], df['Students'], color='skyblue')
5  axs[0].set_title('Number of Students by Major')
6  axs[0].set_xlabel('Major')
7  axs[0].set_ylabel('Number of Students')
8
9  # Line chart
10 axs[1].plot(years, sales, marker='o', color='green')
11 axs[1].set_title('Annual Sales of a Product')
12 axs[1].set_xlabel('Year')
13 axs[1].set_ylabel('Sales (in thousands)')
14 axs[1].grid()
15
16 plt.tight_layout()
17 plt.show()
```

Incorporating Color and Aesthetics

The use of color is an important aspect of data visualization. Color can not only make a visualization more attractive, but it can also help encode information. However, it is important to be mindful of how colors are used:

- **Contrast Color**: Ensure that there is enough contrast between the background and the data to facilitate reading.

- **Color Blindness**: Consider that some people are colorblind and use color palettes that are accessible.

Color Tools

Color palettes can be easily handled in Python using libraries such as `seaborn`. This library provides predefined color palettes that are especially useful for more attractive visualizations.

```
1  import seaborn as sns
2
3  # Example with seaborn
4  sns.set_palette("pastel")
5  plt.bar(df['Major'], df['Students'])
6  plt.title('Number of Students by Major')
7  plt.ylabel('Number of Students')
8  plt.show()
```

Conclusion

Creating effective visualizations is an art that combines clarity, accuracy, and context. Throughout this chapter, we have explored design principles, types of graphs, and best practices for data presentation. By applying these principles, you will be able to communicate your findings more effectively and help your audience better understand the information presented. Remember that a well-designed visualization can be the key to making discoveries and making informed decisions in the field of artificial intelligence.

## Chapter 28

Functional Programming Concepts

Introduction

Functional programming is a programming paradigm that focuses on building programs through the evaluation of functions and avoids the use of mutable state and changing data. Unlike imperative programming, where the steps the program must follow are defined sequentially, functional programming emphasizes the use of functions and applying functions to data. This approach can lead to cleaner code that is easier to maintain and less prone to errors. In this chapter, we will explore the fundamental concepts of functional programming, its practical application in Python, and how it can be particularly useful in the field of artificial intelligence.

Principles of Functional Programming

Immutability

One of the most important principles of functional programming is immutability. Instead of allowing data structures to change over time, new data structures are created as a result of operations. This reduces the likelihood of side effects, meaning the state of the application is more predictable. When working with data sets in artificial intelligence, immutability can help avoid difficult debugging scenarios that often result from unexpected changes in state.

```python
1  # Example of immutability in Python
2  immutable_tuple = (1, 2, 3)
3  # Cannot be modified
4  # immutable_tuple[0] = 10  # This would raise an error
```

First-Class Functions

In functional programming, functions are treated as first-class citizens. This means they can be assigned to variables, passed as arguments to other functions, and returned as results of functions. This capability allows for a higher level of abstraction and facilitates the creation of more complex functions from simpler ones.

```python
1  def add(a, b):
2      return a + b
3
4  def operate(func, x, y):
5      return func(x, y)
```

```
6
7   result = operate(add, 5, 3)  # Calls the add function
8   print(result)  # Output: 8
```

Pure Functions

Pure functions are those that, given a set of inputs, always return the same result and do not cause side effects in the program's state. This means they do not depend on external variables and do not modify data outside their scope. Using pure functions can simplify code testing and debugging.

```
1   def pure_function(x):
2       return x * 2
        # Always returns the same result for the same input
3
4   print(pure_function(4))  # Output: 8
```

Function Composition

Function composition is the process of combining two or more functions into one. Doing this allows building more complex functions from simpler and reusable functions. In Python, we can achieve function composition by defining a new function that calls other functions within it.

```
1   def multiply_by_two(x):
2       return x * 2
3
4   def add_three(x):
5       return x + 3
6
```

```
 7  def composition(func1, func2):
 8      return lambda x: func2(func1(x))
 9
10  new_function = composition(multiply_by_two, add_three)
11  print(new_function(5))  # Output: 13  (5 * 2 + 3)
```

Recursion

Recursion is a technique in functional programming where a function calls itself. This approach is often used to solve problems that can be divided into smaller subproblems. It is essential in situations where there is a need to process data structures like lists or trees.

```
1  def factorial(n):
2      if n == 0:
3          return 1
4      else:
5          return n * factorial(n - 1)
6
7  print(factorial(5))  # Output: 120
```

Functional Programming in Python

Python supports functional programming and provides built-in tools to facilitate the implementation of this paradigm. Some of the most useful tools and functions for working with functional programming in Python are `map()`, `filter()`, and `reduce()`.

Using `map()`

The `map()` function is used to apply a function to all elements of an iterable, such as a list, returning a new iterable with the results. This is a concise way to apply an operation to each element without needing to use an explicit loop.

```python
numbers = [1, 2, 3, 4, 5]

# Using map to double the numbers
doubles = list(map(lambda x: x * 2, numbers))
print(doubles)  # Output: [2, 4, 6, 8, 10]
```

Using `filter()`

The `filter()` function allows filtering elements of an iterable based on a function that returns `True` or `False`. This is useful for creating new lists that only contain elements that meet a condition.

```python
# Filtering even numbers
even_numbers = list(filter(lambda x: x % 2 == 0, numbers))
print(even_numbers)  # Output: [2, 4]
```

Using `reduce()`

The `reduce()` function (available in the `functools` module) applies a function cumulatively to the elements of an iterable, reducing the iterable to a single value.

```
1  from functools import reduce
2
3  # Calculating the product of all numbers
4  product = reduce(lambda x, y: x * y, numbers)
5  print(product)  # Output: 120
```

Advantages of Functional Programming

Functional programming has several advantages that make it appealing, especially in the field of artificial intelligence:

- **Fewer Bugs**: Immutability and the use of pure functions make the code less prone to errors. Side effects are minimized, resulting in a more predictable state.

- **Cleaner Code**: Small, reusable functions allow for greater modularity, making the code easier to read and maintain.

- **Ease for Parallelism**: Due to the nature of immutable data, functional programming facilitates parallel execution, which is essential in artificial intelligence applications requiring intensive processing.

- **Composition**: The ability to compose functions allows for solving complex problems in a more simplified manner and enables code reuse.

Conclusion

Functional programming is a powerful paradigm that offers tools and methods for tackling complex problems in programming, especially in the realm of artificial intelligence. By focusing on pure functions, immutability, and function composition, developers can create cleaner, more maintainable code that is less prone to errors. In this chapter, we have explored the fundamental concepts of functional programming and demonstrated how to implement them using Python. As you advance in your journey in artificial intelligence, considering the use of functional programming techniques can greatly enhance your development skills and your applications.

## Chapter 29

Object-Oriented Programming in Python

Introduction

Object-oriented programming (OOP) is a paradigm that organizes software design around "objects," which are instances of classes. This approach allows grouping related data and behaviors into a single unit, thus facilitating code structuring, reusability, and scalability. OOP is widely used in modern software development, including artificial intelligence systems.

In this chapter, we will explore the fundamental concepts of object-oriented programming through Python, such as classes, objects, inheritance, encapsulation, and polymorphism. We will use practical examples to illustrate how to apply these concepts in the development of more complex applications and systems.

Classes and Objects

Class Definition

A class is a blueprint for creating objects. It defines a set of attributes and methods that will determine the behavior and state of the objects of that class. Think of a class as an architectural blueprint for building a house; it specifies how the house should be, but it is not a house itself.

In Python, we define a class using the `class` keyword. Let's see how to create a simple class called `Car`:

```python
class Car:
    # Constructor of the class
    def __init__(self, brand, model, year):
        self.brand = brand      # Brand attribute
        self.model = model      # Model attribute
        self.year = year        # Year attribute

    # Method to display car information
    def display_info(self):
        print(f"Car: {self.brand} {self.model}, Year: {self.year}")
```

Creating Objects

Once we have a class defined, we can create instances (objects) of that class. Each object can have its own specific attributes and behaviors. Here is how to create an object using the `Car` class:

```
1  # Creating instances of the Car class
2  car1 = Car("Toyota", "Corolla", 2020)
3  car2 = Car("Honda", "Civic", 2021)
4
5  # Displaying information about the cars
6  car1.display_info()
7  car2.display_info()
```

Attributes and Methods

Attributes are the properties of an object; they are the variables it stores. Methods are functions associated with a class that define its behavior. In our Car class example, brand, model, and year are attributes, while display_info is a method.

Inheritance

Inheritance is a key concept in OOP that allows a class to acquire characteristics (attributes and methods) from another class. This relationship is referred to as a "parent-child relationship." The class that inherits is called a **subclass** or **derived class**, and the class from which it inherits is called a **superclass** or **base class**.

Inheritance Example

Let's consider that we want to create a new class called ElectricCar, which inherits from the Car class. This will allow us to reuse the attributes and methods of Car without duplicating code.

```
1   class ElectricCar(Car):  # Inheriting from Car
2       def __init__(self, brand, model, year, range):
3           super().__init__(brand, model, year)
        # Calling the superclass constructor
4           self.range = range
        # Specific attribute for ElectricCar
5
6       def display_info(self):
7           super().display_info()
        # Calling the superclass method
8           print(f"Range: {self.range} km")
```

Here, the `ElectricCar` class inherits the properties and methods of the `Car` class but also introduces an additional attribute: `range`.

```
1   # Creating an instance of ElectricCar
2   electric_car = ElectricCar("Tesla", "Model 3", 2022, 500)
3   electric_car.display_info()
```

Encapsulation

Encapsulation is the process of hiding the internal details of a class and exposing only what is necessary to users. It is used to protect the data of a class. In Python, this can be achieved using naming conventions for attributes.

Private Attributes

We can define attributes as private by prefixing an underscore (_) to their name. This indicates that these attributes should not be accessed from outside the class.

```
1   class Car:
2       def __init__(self, brand, model, year):
3           self._brand = brand        # Private attribute
4           self._model = model
5           self._year = year
6
7       def display_info(self):
8           print(f"Car: {self._brand} {self._model}, Year: {self._year}")
9
10  # Creating a car
11  car = Car("Ford", "Fiesta", 2019)
12  car.display_info()
13
        # print(car._brand)  # This is not recommended and could be
        problematic
```

Access Methods (Getters and Setters)

To manipulate private attributes, we can implement access methods (getters) and methods to modify them (setters).

```
1   class Car:
2       def __init__(self, brand, model, year):
3           self._brand = brand
4           self._model = model
5           self._year = year
6
7       def get_brand(self):
8           return self._brand
9
10      def set_brand(self, new_brand):
11          self._brand = new_brand
```

Now, we can access the _brand attribute in a controlled manner:

```
1  car = Car("Ford", "Fiesta", 2019)
2  print(car.get_brand())  # Accessing _brand through the getter
3  car.set_brand("Chevrolet")
     # Modifying _brand through the setter
4  print(car.get_brand())
```

Polymorphism

Polymorphism allows methods with the same name to be used across different classes. This is useful in data structures where different types of objects can be grouped together, yet the same method can still be called.

Polymorphism Example

Continuing the example of the Car class and its subclass ElectricCar, both have a display_info() method, but their implementations are different. This allows the user to call display_info() on an object of either class, and the correct behavior will be determined at runtime.

```
1  def show_information(car):
2      car.display_info()  # Here, polymorphism is applied
3
4  # Creating a car and an electric car
5  car1 = Car("Honda", "Civic", 2020)
6  car2 = ElectricCar("Tesla", "Model 3", 2022, 500)
7
8  # Displaying information about both
9  show_information(car1)
10 show_information(car2)
```

Conclusion

Object-oriented programming is a powerful paradigm that organizes code in a modular and reusable way. Through understanding fundamental concepts such as classes, objects, inheritance, encapsulation, and polymorphism, developers can create systems that are easier to maintain, extend, and understand.

In this chapter, we have explored object-oriented programming in Python, applying these ideas to concrete examples. As you progress in your artificial intelligence projects, understanding and applying these principles will enable you to create more robust and flexible systems that adapt to your needs. Object-oriented programming is an invaluable tool in any developer's arsenal, and mastering it will come with practice and application in real-world contexts.

## Chapter 30

Integrating Programming Styles

Introduction

In software development, the choice of programming style is fundamental, as it influences the clarity, maintainability, and scalability of the code. In Python, developers have the flexibility to adopt different paradigms, with the most prominent being functional programming and object-oriented programming. The integration of these paradigms is a powerful strategy that allows for the creation of more robust and reusable code. In this chapter, we will explore how to combine functional programming and object-oriented programming in Python, and how to make use of best practices to maintain clean and optimized code.

Understanding Programming Paradigms

Functional Programming

Functional programming is based on the use of pure functions, immutability, and the application of functions as first-class citizens. This approach promotes the use of functions as building blocks of software, avoiding side effects and providing more predictable and straightforward code.

Object-Oriented Programming

On the other hand, object-oriented programming focuses on the creation of objects that encapsulate both data (attributes) and behaviors (methods). This paradigm is especially useful in larger and more complex projects, as it allows for the representation of real-world entities and their interactions through classes and objects.

Advantages of Style Integration

The combination of functional and object-oriented programming in Python offers several advantages:

- **Flexibility**: It allows developers to select the most appropriate style for a specific task, improving the efficiency of the code.

- **Code Reusability**: Independent functions can be created and used within classes, enhancing modularity.

- **Improved Readability**: Using a mixed approach can make the code more concise and easier to follow, especially in complex applications.

Practical Example: Library Manager

To illustrate the integration of programming styles, we will create a library manager that uses classes to represent books and functions to perform operations on them.

Definition of the Book Class

First, we define a Book class that will contain basic attributes to describe a book:

```python
class Book:
    def __init__(self, title, author, publication_year):
        self.title = title
        self.author = author
        self.publication_year = publication_year
        self.borrowed = False

    def show_info(self):
        status = "Borrowed" if self.borrowed else "Available"
        return f"{self.title} by {self.author} ({self.publication_year}) - {status}"
```

Here, the Book class has a show_info method that returns a string representation of the object.

Functions to Manage Books

Next, we implement functions that operate on a list of books. These functions will benefit from the functional nature as they will not directly modify the objects in the list.

Function to Filter Available Books

Let's create a function that filters the available books in the library:

```
1  def available_books(library):
2      return list(filter(lambda book: not book.borrowed,
       library))
```

This function uses `filter()` to return only those books that are not borrowed.

Function to Borrow a Book

Now, let's implement a function that allows users to borrow a book:

```
1  def borrow_book(title, library):
2      for book in library:
3          if book.title == title and not book.borrowed:
4              book.borrowed = True
5              return f"You have borrowed '{title}'."
6      return f"The book '{title}' is not available."
```

This function performs a linear search through the books in the library and sets the `borrowed` status to `True` if the requested book is found.

Integrating Functions into Classes

Sometimes, it is useful to include functions in classes as class methods. This can help manage the state of objects more conveniently. To illustrate this point, let's add a `make_borrow` method to the `Book` class.

```
1  class Book:
2      # Constructor and show_info method remain the same
3
4      def make_borrow(self):
5          if self.borrowed:
6              return f"{self.title} is already borrowed."
7          else:
8              self.borrowed = True
9              return f"{self.title} has been borrowed."
```

Using the Library Manager

Now that we have our class and functions defined, let's see how we can use this system in practice:

```
1  # Creating a list of books
2  library = [
3      Book("One Hundred Years of Solitude",
   "Gabriel García Márquez", 1967),
4      Book("1984", "George Orwell", 1949),
5      Book("The Little Prince", "Antoine de Saint-Exupéry",
   1943),
6  ]
7
8  # Showing information of all books
9  for book in library:
10     print(book.show_info())
11
12 # Filtering available books
13 available = available_books(library)
14 print("\nAvailable books:")
15 for book in available:
16     print(book.show_info())
```

```
17
18  # Borrowing a book
19  print(borrow_book("1984", library))
20
21  # Showing information of all books again
22  for book in library:
23      print(book.show_info())
```

In this example, we have created a simple library that combines object-oriented programming (through the `Book` class) and functional programming (through the use of functions like `available_books` and `borrow_book`).

Best Practices for Clean Code

When integrating different programming styles, it is important to follow certain best practices:

- **Documentation**: Commenting the code and explaining functions and methods will help others (and yourself in the future) to quickly understand the purpose of the code.

- **Naming Conventions**: Use consistent and descriptive naming conventions for functions, classes, and attributes.

- **Separation of Concerns**: Keep class functionalities and functions independent to improve modularity and maintainability.

- **Minimalism**: Avoid creating unnecessary functions or classes; each should have a clear responsibility.

Conclusion

The integration of programming styles in Python, specifically the combination of object-oriented programming and functional programming, allows developers to leverage the best of both worlds. By using classes to represent entities and functions to operate on them, clearer, cleaner, and more efficient code can be developed. As you continue to explore this chapter as part of your training in artificial intelligence, remember that flexibility in your programming approach can give you a significant advantage when tackling complex problems.

## Chapter 31

Introduction to Parallel Programming

Introduction

Parallel programming is an approach that enables the simultaneous execution of multiple operations on different processor cores, thus improving efficiency and reducing processing time compared to sequential execution. As problems become more complex and data volumes increase, the ability to parallelize processes becomes essential, especially in fields like artificial intelligence, where processing large datasets is common.

In this chapter, we will explore the basic concepts of parallel programming, its benefits, the tools available in Python for implementing parallelization, and some practical applications in the context of artificial intelligence.

Why Use Parallel Programming

Advantages of Parallel Programming

- **Performance Improvement**: Dividing a problem into smaller tasks that can be executed simultaneously reduces the overall processing time.

- **Resource Efficiency**: By leveraging multiple processor cores, hardware resources are optimized, resulting in better utilization of available processing capacity.

- **Scalability**: Parallel programming allows an application to scale effectively by utilizing more hardware, such as multiple processors or machines on a network.

- **Handling Large Volumes of Data**: For tasks like machine learning and manipulation of large datasets, parallelization can accelerate model training.

Basic Concepts of Parallel Programming

Parallel programming can be implemented in several ways, including:

- **Data-Level Parallelism**: This occurs when different parts of a dataset are processed simultaneously. It is particularly useful in matrix operations and numerical computations.

- **Task-Level Parallelism**: This involves dividing a problem into independent tasks that can be executed concurrently. This is beneficial in applications where different tasks do not depend on each other.

- **Execution Dedication Parallelism**: This refers to assigning distinct tasks to different processors, allowing each to execute its own set of instructions.

Parallel Programming Tools in Python

Python provides several libraries and tools that facilitate the implementation of parallel programming. Below, we will explore some of the most popular ones.

1. Multithreading with `threading`

Python includes the `threading` module, which allows for the creation and management of threads. This approach is useful for tasks that do not require significant computational power and where waiting time, such as input/output (I/O) operations, can be used efficiently.

Example of Using the `threading` Module

In this example, we will see how to use threads to perform simultaneous tasks.

```python
import threading
import time

def task(name):
    for i in range(5):
        print(f"Task {name} is running...")
        time.sleep(1)

```

```
 9   # Create threads
10   thread1 = threading.Thread(target=task, args=("A",))
11   thread2 = threading.Thread(target=task, args=("B",))
12
13   # Start threads
14   thread1.start()
15   thread2.start()
16
17   # Wait for them to finish
18   thread1.join()
19   thread2.join()
20
21   print("Tasks completed.")
```

In this example, two threads are created that execute the `task` function simultaneously. This allows both tasks to be performed at the same time during the allocated duration.

2. Multiprocessing with `multiprocessing`

The `multiprocessing` module provides a more powerful alternative to the `threading` module, allowing the creation of independent processes that run in their own memory space. This is particularly useful when seeking to leverage parallelism in tasks that require high computational performance.

Example of Using the `multiprocessing` Module

Next, we will examine how to use `multiprocessing` to execute functions in parallel.

```python
1   import multiprocessing
2   import time
3
4   def task(name):
5       for i in range(5):
6           print(f"Task {name} is running...")
7           time.sleep(1)
8
9   if __name__ == '__main__':
10      # Create processes
11      process1 = multiprocessing.Process(target=task, args=(
    "A",))
12      process2 = multiprocessing.Process(target=task, args=(
    "B",))
13
14      # Start processes
15      process1.start()
16      process2.start()
17
18      # Wait for them to finish
19      process1.join()
20      process2.join()
21
22      print("Tasks completed.")
```

In this case, processes are used instead of threads. Each process has its own memory space, which eliminates concurrency issues that may arise with threads in Python.

3. Using `concurrent.futures`

The `concurrent.futures` library provides a high-level interface for executing tasks in parallel in an easy-to-use manner. It offers two main classes: `ThreadPoolExecutor` for thread execution and

`ProcessPoolExecutor` for process execution.

Example with `ThreadPoolExecutor`

```python
1   from concurrent.futures import ThreadPoolExecutor
2   import time
3
4   def task(name):
5       for i in range(5):
6           print(f"Task {name} is running...")
7           time.sleep(1)
8
9   with ThreadPoolExecutor(max_workers=2) as executor:
10      executor.submit(task, "A")
11      executor.submit(task, "B")
12
13  print("Tasks completed.")
```

In this example, `ThreadPoolExecutor` is used to execute two tasks simultaneously, simplifying thread creation and tracking their completion.

Practical Example: Parallel Training of an AI Model

In the context of artificial intelligence, model training can significantly benefit from parallelization. Imagine that we have a very large dataset and we want to train multiple models simultaneously to find the best performance.

```python
1   from concurrent.futures import ProcessPoolExecutor
2   import numpy as np
3
4   def train_model(dataset):
```

```
5      # Simulating model training
6      time.sleep(2)
7      return f"Model trained with {len(dataset)} samples"
8
9  # Simulating datasets
10 datasets = [np.random.rand(1000, 10) for _ in range(5)]
11
12 with ProcessPoolExecutor() as executor:
13     results = executor.map(train_model, datasets)
14
15 for result in results:
16     print(result)
```

In this case, we simulate the training of models on different datasets using `ProcessPoolExecutor`. Each dataset is trained in a separate process, allowing for more efficient use of training time.

Conclusion

Parallel programming is an invaluable technique in the realm of software development and artificial intelligence, allowing for the maximization of available resources and the improvement of processing efficiency. The various tools and approaches to parallelization in Python, such as `threading`, `multiprocessing`, and `concurrent.futures`, provide developers with the necessary flexibility to implement scalable solutions. As datasets and models become more complex, mastering these techniques will be crucial to keeping pace with the evolution of artificial intelligence and data analysis. With the right knowledge and practice, programmers will be able to integrate parallelization strategies into their projects, thereby optimizing performance and efficacy.

## Chapter 32

Code Structuring and Organization

Introduction

The quality of code in any programming project is a determining factor in its maintainability and scalability. As projects grow in size and complexity, the structure of that code becomes even more crucial. Good organization helps developers not only understand and manage their own work but also collaborate more effectively with others. In this chapter, we will explore best practices for structuring and organizing code in Python, including concepts of modularization, encapsulation, use of packages and modules, as well as the importance of proper documentation.

The Importance of Good Structuring

A well-organized code structure facilitates:

- **Maintainability**: Clear and well-organized code is easier to modify and update over time.

- **Reusability**: Modularization allows components and functions to be reused in different parts of a project or in future projects.

- **Collaboration**: Organized code is easier for other developers to understand, improving collaboration in teams.

- **Scalability**: As new features or functionalities are added, well-structured code can be easily expanded instead of becoming a chaotic puzzle.

Basic Principles of Code Organization

Modularization

Modularization refers to dividing a program into separate and autonomous modules. A module in Python is simply a file that contains Python definitions and statements. Below are some essential principles to follow when modularizing code:

- **Cohesion**: Each module should focus on a single responsibility or a related set of functions. This makes it easier to understand and reuse.

- **Coupling**: Modules should be as loosely interconnected as possible. This means they should depend on other modules minimally and in a controlled manner, thus facilitating future changes.

Example of a Simple Module

```
1  # calculations_module.py
2  def add(a, b):
3      return a + b
4
5  def subtract(a, b):
6      return a - b
```

In this example, `calculations_module.py` contains all related mathematical operations, making it easy to understand and reuse in other programs.

Use of Packages

In Python, a package is a way of structuring modules. A package is simply a directory that contains multiple modules and a special file called `__init__.py`, which indicates to Python that the directory should be treated as a package.

```
1  my_package/
2      __init__.py
3      calculations_module.py
4      plotting_module.py
```

With this structure, we can import the modules using:

```
1  from my_package import calculations_module
2  result = calculations_module.add(5, 3)
3  print(result)  # Output: 8
```

Encapsulation of Functions

Encapsulation is a principle that involves hiding the internal implementation of a module or class. This is done to protect the object's state and avoid undesired modifications from the outside. In Python, while there is no true private encapsulation as in other languages, we can follow certain conventions.

- **Private Attributes**: Prefixing an attribute name with an underscore (_) indicates that it is a convention of non-public access.

Example of Encapsulation in a Class

```
1   class Counter:
2       def __init__(self):
3           self._count = 0  # 'Private' attribute
4
5       def increment(self):
6           self._count += 1
7
8       def show_count(self):
9           return self._count
```

In the code above, the attribute _count is considered internal and should not be modified directly from outside the class.

Code Documentation

Documentation is a critical part of code organization that is often overlooked, but its importance cannot be underestimated. Code without documentation can be extremely difficult to understand and maintain. Below are some best practices for documenting code in Python:

- **Docstrings**: Use documentation strings to describe the functionality of modules, classes, and methods. This allows other developers (or yourself in the future) to easily understand what the code does.

```
1  def add(a, b):
2      """
3      Adds two numbers.
4
5      Parameters:
6      a (int): The first number.
7      b (int): The second number.
8
9      Returns:
10     int: The sum of a and b.
11     """
12     return a + b
```

- **Comments**: In addition to docstrings, it is useful to include inline comments explaining sections of code that may not be immediately obvious.

Code Style

Following a consistent coding style is vital for maintaining good organization. In Python, it is recommended to adhere to the **PEP 8** guidelines, which is the official style guide for Python. Some of the recommendations from PEP 8 include:

- Use whitespace consistently.

- Follow the case convention for naming (e.g., `snake_case` for functions and variables).

- Lines of code should not exceed 79 characters.

- Leave a blank line between functions and classes to improve readability.

Tools for Code Organization

Version Control

Using version control, such as **Git**, is fundamental for organizing code in software projects. It allows for tracking changes in the code, collaborating with other developers, and reverting changes when necessary. With Git, you can create branches to work on new features without affecting the main version of the code.

Folder Structure

A proper folder structure is crucial in any project. Here is an example of what a project structure could look like:

```
my_project/
    ├── src/
    │   ├── __init__.py
    │   ├── calculations_module.py
    │   └── plotting_module.py
    ├── tests/
    │   ├── test_calculations_module.py
    │   └── test_plotting_module.py
    ├── README.md
    └── requirements.txt
```

- `src/`: Folder containing the source code.

- `tests/`: Folder including unit tests.

- `README.md`: Documentation for the project.

- `requirements.txt`: List of dependencies for the project.

Use of Virtual Environments

Using virtual environments is a recommended practice that allows you to manage your project's dependencies without interfering with other projects. You can create a virtual environment using `venv` or `conda` to ensure that the libraries you are using are isolated.

```
1  # Create a virtual environment
2  python -m venv my_virtual_env
3
4  # Activate the virtual environment on Windows
5  my_virtual_env\Scripts\activate
6
7  # Activate the virtual environment on macOS/Linux
8  source my_virtual_env/bin/activate
```

Conclusion

The structuring and organization of code is a fundamental aspect of software development that not only affects the quality of the final product but also influences the developer's experience. By adopting principles of modularization, encapsulation, documentation, and following good style practices, you can create cleaner, more maintainable, and scalable code. As you continue your journey in programming and in the field of artificial intelligence, attention to code organization will be an invaluable asset that will serve you throughout your career.

## Chapter 33

Debugging and Error Handling

Introduction

Debugging and error handling are critical aspects of software development, and their importance increases significantly in artificial intelligence projects where errors can be difficult to trace and fix. Debugging helps developers identify and correct bugs in the code, while proper error handling ensures that the application is robust and resilient, even when unexpected situations arise. In this chapter, we will explore debugging techniques and effective strategies for handling errors in Python.

The Importance of Debugging

Debugging is the process of identifying and correcting errors or "bugs" in the code. These errors can come in various forms, including:

- **Syntax Errors**: Errors that prevent the code from running, such as forgetting to close a parenthesis or using a wrong keyword.

- **Runtime Errors**: Occur during the execution of the program, such as attempting to divide by zero or referencing an undefined variable.

- **Logical Errors**: Result in incorrect behavior of the program, even though there are no syntax or runtime errors. For example, incorrectly calculating an expected result.

Effective debugging not only resolves immediate issues but also improves the overall quality of the code, increases developer productivity, and ultimately provides a better user experience.

Debugging Strategies

Reading and Understanding the Code

Before diving into debugging tools, it is essential to read and understand the code. Often, errors can be obvious by simply reviewing the problematic lines. Take some time to reflect on how the code should function.

Using Print Statements

A common and effective debugging technique is the use of print statements. By adding strategic print statements, you can observe how the program behaves at different points during its execution.

```
1   def calculate_average(numbers):
```

```
2        total = sum(numbers)
3        average = total / len(numbers)
4        print(f"Total: {total}, Average: {average}")
       # Print statement
5        return average
6
7   result = calculate_average([10, 20, 30])
```

In this example, the print statements allow you to check the values of `total` and `average` before they are returned.

Using a Debugger

Python has a built-in debugger called `pdb` (Python Debugger), which provides a powerful way to interact with the code at runtime. You can set breakpoints, inspect variables, and execute the code line by line.

Example of Using `pdb`

To use `pdb`, you first need to import the module and then set a breakpoint in the code.

```
1   import pdb
2
3   def divide(a, b):
4       pdb.set_trace()  # Set a breakpoint
5       return a / b
6
7   result = divide(10, 0)  # This will raise an error
```

When you run this code, it will stop at `pdb.set_trace()`, allowing you to interact with the environment. You can inspect current variables, execute commands (like n for the next line or c to continue), and observe how your program behaves in real-time.

Assertions

Assertions are another useful debugging method. They allow you to verify that certain conditions hold true during the execution of your code.

```
1  def square_root(x):
2      assert x >= 0, "The number must be non-negative"
3      return x ** 0.5
4
5  square_root(-10)  # This will raise an assertion error
```

If x is negative, the assertion will fail and raise an exception, indicating which condition was not met.

Error Handling in Python

Error handling refers to how your program responds to unexpected conditions or errors during its execution. In Python, this is done using try and except blocks.

Using try and except

You can enclose code that might cause an error in a try block and handle the error in an except block.

```
1  def divide(a, b):
2      try:
3          result = a / b
4      except ZeroDivisionError:
5          print("Error: Cannot divide by zero.")
6          return None
7      return result
8
9  result = divide(10, 0)  # This will not cause a crash
10 print(result)  # Output: Error: Cannot divide by zero.
```

In this example, if a zero division error occurs, instead of crashing the program, the exception is caught, and an informative message is printed.

Multiple Exceptions

You can also handle multiple exceptions in a single except block or have several except blocks for different types of errors.

```
1  def process_data(data):
2      try:
3          result = data["key1"] / data["key2"]
4      except KeyError:
5          print("Error: Missing a required key in the data.")
6          return None
7      except ZeroDivisionError:
8          print("Error: Division by zero.")
9          return None
10     return result
11
12 data = {"key1": 10, "key2": 0}
13 result = process_data(data)  # Catches the ZeroDivisionError
14 print(result)
```

297

Using `else` and `finally`

Python also allows the use of `else` and `finally` with `try` and `except` blocks. The `else` block is executed if no exception occurs, while the `finally` block is always executed, regardless of whether an error occurred.

```python
def divide(a, b):
    try:
        result = a / b
    except ZeroDivisionError:
        print("Error: Cannot divide by zero.")
        return None
    else:
        print("Division was successful.")
        return result
    finally:
        print("Finalizing the division operation.")

result = divide(10, 2)
print(result)
```

In this case, the `finally` block is used to perform cleanup actions, such as releasing resources, closing connections, or printing final messages.

Conclusion

Debugging and error handling are essential skills in programming and are particularly important in developing artificial intelligence systems, where large volumes of data are handled and complex calculations are performed. Through effective debugging techniques, such as using print statements, debugging tools, and assertions, developers can identify and correct errors more efficiently.

Moreover, proper use of `try` and `except` blocks allows applications to handle errors gracefully and maintain a smooth user experience. Mastering these skills will not only improve the quality of your code but also boost your confidence as a developer, preparing you to tackle more ambitious projects in the field of artificial intelligence.

## Chapter 34

Optimization and Performance Improvement

Introduction

Optimization and performance improvement are crucial aspects of software development, especially in applications that require intensive processing, such as artificial intelligence systems. As programs grow in complexity and handle ever-increasing volumes of data, the efficiency of the code becomes a determining factor to ensure that time and resource requirements are met. In this chapter, we will explore various strategies and techniques to optimize the performance of applications in Python, from identifying bottlenecks to implementing effective solutions that enhance efficiency.

Understanding Program Performance

Before diving into optimization, it is important to understand what performance means in the context of a program. Generally, performance can be measured in terms of:

- **Execution Time**: How long it takes for a program to complete its task.

- **Resource Usage**: How much memory, CPU, disk, or network is utilized during its execution.

Performance improvement seeks to reduce execution time and minimize resource usage, ensuring that the program runs more efficiently and effectively.

Identifying Bottlenecks

The first step in the optimization process is to identify bottlenecks, which are those parts of the program that limit overall performance. To do this, we employ performance analysis and monitoring tools that allow us to locate where delays occur.

Profiling

Profiling is a technique used to measure the time taken by each part of a program. Python has several built-in tools that make this task easier, with `cProfile` and `timeit` being two of the most useful.

Using `cProfile`

The `cProfile` library allows you to obtain a detailed report of the time spent in each function of a program. Below is an example of how to use `cProfile` to analyze the performance of a piece of code:

```
1  import cProfile
2
3  def expensive_function():
4      total = 0
5      for i in range(10000):
6          total += sum(range(100))
7      return total
8
9  cProfile.run('expensive_function()')
```

This code will execute `expensive_function` and print a report on the time spent in each called function, allowing you to identify which one is responsible for the most time consumption.

Using `timeit`

Another useful tool is `timeit`, which is designed to measure the execution time of small code snippets. It is especially helpful when you want to make comparisons between different implementations.

```
1  import timeit
2
3  def list_sum():
4      return sum(range(100))
5
```

```
6  time = timeit.timeit(list_sum, number=10000)
7  print(f"Execution time: {time}")
```

Here, `timeit` runs the `list_sum` function 10,000 times, returning the total time it took, giving you an accurate idea of its performance.

Optimization Strategies

Once you have identified the bottlenecks in your code, you can apply various strategies to improve performance.

Algorithmic Improvements

Switching to a more efficient algorithm can have a radical impact on performance. Ensure that you address the time complexity of your algorithms, as algorithms with `O(n)` or `O(log n)` notation will generally execute faster than those with `O(n^2)`.

Example of Algorithmic Improvement

Suppose you have a search problem in a list. Using linear search has a complexity of `O(n)`, while binary search has a complexity of `O(log n)`. Switching to binary search after sorting the list can significantly enhance efficiency:

```
1  # Linear Search
2  def linear_search(lst, target):
3      for index, value in enumerate(lst):
4          if value == target:
```

```
5                   return index
6         return -1
7
8  # Binary Search
9  def binary_search(lst, target):
10         left, right = 0, len(lst) - 1
11         while left <= right:
12             mid = (left + right) // 2
13             if lst[mid] == target:
14                 return mid
15             elif lst[mid] < target:
16                 left = mid + 1
17             else:
18                 right = mid - 1
19         return -1
```

Using Generators and Comprehensions

Python supports generators, which are an efficient way to handle large amounts of data. Instead of generating a complete list, a generator produces elements one at a time and consumes them on demand, saving memory.

Using Generators

```
1  def generator():
2      for i in range(1000000):
3          yield i * 2
4
5  for number in generator():
6      print(number)
```

```
# This will not load the entire list into memory
```

I/O (Input/Output) Optimization

Programs that perform multiple I/O operations can be a significant hindrance to performance. Here are some strategies to optimize I/O operations:

- **Reading files in chunks**: Instead of reading large files line-by-line, consider reading them in chunks.
- **Using efficient libraries**: Utilize libraries like `pandas` for data manipulation, as they are optimized for these tasks.

Using C Libraries and Extensions

If you need even higher performance, you can consider writing critical parts of your code in C or using C extensions, such as Cython. This is particularly useful for intensive numerical calculations that can benefit from C's speed.

Example of Cython

Using Cython, you can compile Python code to C code:

```
1  # cython: language_level=3
2  def cython_sum(int n):
3      cdef int total = 0
4      for i in range(n):
5          total += i
6      return total
```

Concurrency and Parallelism

For applications that require high performance and involve tasks that can be executed concurrently, considering the incorporation of parallel or concurrent programming can help.

- **Multiprocessing**: Use the `multiprocessing` module to run functions in parallel across multiple processor cores.

```python
from multiprocessing import Pool

def expensive_function(x):
    return sum(i * i for i in range(x))

if __name__ == '__main__':
    with Pool(4) as p:  # Use 4 processes
        results = p.map(expensive_function, [1000000] * 4)
```

Performance Evaluation

Finally, after implementing optimizations, it is vital to review and evaluate the performance again. Use `cProfile` and `timeit` to check if the improvements have resulted in superior performance.

Conclusion

Optimization and performance improvement are essential in developing efficient software, especially in the context of artificial intelligence and data processing. Identifying bottlenecks, applying appropriate optimization strategies, and evaluating performance are crucial steps in creating fast and effective applications. With a conscious and methodical approach to optimization, you can turn basic software into a robust solution capable of handling the complexity and data volume demanded by modern artificial intelligence applications.

## Chapter 35

Documentation and Code Maintenance

Introduction

Documentation and code maintenance are vital components for the success of any software project. As developers work on code over time, it is crucial that both they and any other collaborators can easily understand how the system works. This chapter explores the importance of proper documentation, tools and techniques for creating effective documentation, as well as best practices for maintenance throughout the software lifecycle.

The Importance of Documentation

Documentation serves as a map that guides developers through the code. Without clear documentation, a project can become unintelligible, especially as it grows in complexity or when new members join the team. Some benefits of good documentation include:

- **Clarity**: Facilitates understanding of the purpose and logic behind each part of the code.

- **Facilitates Onboarding**: Helps new developers quickly adjust to the project by providing them with a clear context on how to use and modify the existing code.

- **Improves Maintainability**: Well-documented code is easier to modify, debug, and expand. This leads to fewer errors and more agile development.

- **Enhances Collaboration**: Facilitates collaboration among team members, as everyone has access to the same information.

Types of Documentation

There are various types of documentation that can be useful in a software project, each serving a specific function:

Code Documentation

This type of documentation includes comments and docstrings within the code. Be sure to comment on code that may not be intuitive at first glance. Docstrings are especially useful because they explain the purpose and use of a function, class, or module.

```
1  def add(a, b):
2      """
3      Adds two numbers.
4
5      Parameters:
```

```
6      a (int): The first number.
7      b (int): The second number.
8
9      Returns:
10     int: The sum of a and b.
11     """
12     return a + b
```

Technical Documentation

Includes details about the system architecture, data flow diagrams, and database structures. This documentation helps developers understand how all the pieces of the system fit together.

User Guides

Aimed at end users, these guides explain how to interact with the software, its features, and functionalities. They should be clear and easy to follow.

Installation Manuals

Instructions on how to install and configure the software in different development environments. This type of documentation is especially useful for new users and developers.

Changelog

A file that documents the changes made in each version of the software. This record is important for maintenance and to inform users about new features, fixes, and improvements.

Tools for Documenting Code

Using the right tools can facilitate the documentation process. Here are some that may be helpful:

Sphinx

Sphinx is a popular tool for generating documentation from docstrings in Python. It allows you to create documentation in HTML, PDF, and other formats.

```
1  pip install sphinx
```

Once installed, you can initialize a project with the command:

```
1  sphinx-quickstart
```

MkDocs

MkDocs is a lighter option that allows you to create project documentation based on Markdown files. It is especially useful for smaller or less complex projects.

```
1  pip install mkdocs
```

To start a project, you can use:

```
1  mkdocs new project_name
```

Jupyter Notebooks

For documentation of data science-related projects, Jupyter Notebooks is a powerful tool that allows you to combine code, visualizations, and explanatory text in a single document.

Best Practices for Documentation

To ensure the effectiveness of documentation, consider the following best practices:

Keep Documentation Up to Date

Outdated documentation can be more harmful than the absence of documentation. Establish procedures to update the documentation whenever you make significant changes to the code.

Be Clear and Concise

Avoid unnecessary jargon. Documentation should be accessible and understandable for people with varying levels of experience. Use practical examples whenever possible.

Organize Information

Divide documentation into well-defined sections using headings and subheadings. This makes navigation easier and allows users to quickly find the information they need.

Use Consistent Formats

Maintain a uniform format throughout the documentation. This includes nomenclature, style, and structure. Use automatic formatting tools if necessary.

Include Examples

Providing code examples can be extremely helpful in clarifying how functions and methods should be used, which reduces the learning curve.

Code Maintenance

Code maintenance is the process of making changes, updates, and improvements to software throughout its lifecycle. Just as documentation plays a crucial role, maintenance is also essential for maintaining quality over time.

Maintenance Strategies

Refactoring

Refactoring is the process of restructuring existing code without altering its external behavior. This can include improving readability, eliminating redundancies, and optimizing data structures.

Automated Testing

Creating automated tests is essential to ensure that modifications to the code do not introduce errors. Unit, integration, and functional tests should be part of the maintenance workflow.

Clean Code

The practice of maintaining clean and well-organized code makes maintenance easier. Use SOLID principles and follow design patterns that allow the code to be understandable and extensible.

Version Control

Using version control systems, such as Git, is essential for code maintenance. It allows you to track changes, collaborate with others, and revert modifications if necessary.

Conclusion

Documentation and code maintenance are critical aspects that should not be overlooked in software development. Good documentation not only enhances the developer experience, but it also allows the software to evolve and be maintained over time. Establishing clear and effective documentation practices, along with solid maintenance strategies, will ensure that the code remains relevant, usable, and high quality. By investing time and effort in these areas, you will lay the groundwork for successful and sustainable software development in the long run.

## Chapter 36

Version Control with Git

Introduction

Version control is an essential practice in modern software development that allows developers to manage changes to the source code over time. Git, one of the most widely used version control tools, not only facilitates collaboration among multiple developers but also helps maintain a clear history of all modifications made in a project. In this chapter, we will explore the basics of Git, how to set it up and use it, as well as some best practices for effective version control management.

What is Git?

Git is a distributed version control system that enables developers to work collaboratively and efficiently on projects. Unlike centralized version control systems, where there is a single main repository, Git allows each developer to have their own complete copy of the repository, facilitating offline work and improving the speed of operations.

Benefits of Using Git

- **Simplified Collaboration**: Multiple people can work on the same project simultaneously without interfering with each other's work.

- **Change History**: Git maintains a complete history of all modifications, allowing developers to trace who changed what and when.

- **Easy Integration**: Git easily integrates with collaborative development platforms like GitHub, GitLab, and Bitbucket, enabling even smoother collaboration.

- **Branches and Merging**: Git allows the creation of "branches" to develop new features without affecting the main version of the code, simplifying the management and release of new functionalities.

Installing Git

Installing Git is a straightforward process that varies slightly depending on the operating system you are using.

Windows

1. Download the installer from the Git website: git-scm.com.

2. Run the installer and follow the installation process.

3. Make sure to add Git to the PATH environment variable during installation, which will allow you to use it from the command line.

macOS

You can install Git via Homebrew, a package manager:

```
1  brew install git
```

Alternatively, you can also download the installer from the official website.

Linux

On most Linux distributions, Git can be installed using the corresponding package manager. For example, on Ubuntu:

```
1  sudo apt-get install git
```

Configuring Git

Once installed, it's essential to configure Git with your personal information to associate it with your commits. You can do this via the command line:

```
1  git config --global user.name "Your Name"
2  git config --global user.email "your.email@example.com"
```

This ensures that any commit you make includes your name and email address.

To verify your configuration, you can use:

```
1  git config --list
```

Creating a Git Repository

A Git repository is where all the project's files and their change history are stored. There are two main ways to create a repository.

Initializing a New Repository

To start a new project, navigate to the project folder and run:

```
1  git init
```

This creates a new empty Git repository in that folder.

Cloning an Existing Repository

If you want to work on an existing project, you can clone a remote repository:

```
1  git clone <repository_url>
```

This creates a local copy of the repository on your machine.

Making Changes and Commits

Once you have your repository, you can start making changes to the files.

Git follows a simple workflow: modify the files, add the changes to the staging area, and then commit.

Modifying Files

Make changes to your files as you normally would. You can use any text editor or IDE.

Adding Changes to the Staging Area

To prepare the changes you've made to be committed, you need to add them to the staging area:

```
1  git add <file_name>
```

If you want to add all changes in the current folder:

```
1  git add .
```

Making a Commit

After adding the files to the staging area, you can make a commit to save the changes:

```
1  git commit -m "Brief description of changes"
```

It's important that the commit message is clear and descriptive, as this will help you and others understand the changes made.

Branches in Git

Branches are a powerful feature of Git that allows you to develop features in isolation from the main code. This is especially useful when working on new features or bug fixes.

Creating a Branch

To create a new branch, you can use:

```
1   git branch <branch_name>
```

Switching Branches

To switch to a different branch:

```
1   git checkout <branch_name>
```

You can also create and switch to a new branch in one step by using:

```
1   git checkout -b <branch_name>
```

Merging Branches

Once you've finished working on a branch, you can merge the changes back into the main branch (often called main or master):

1. Switch to the main branch:

```
1  git checkout main
```

2. Merge the branch you want to incorporate:

```
1  git merge <branch_name>
```

Resolving Conflicts

When merging branches, there may be conflicts if two branches have modified the same lines in a file. Git will alert you to these conflicts, and you must resolve them manually.

1. Open the conflicting files and look for the sections marked with <<<<<<<, =======, and >>>>>>>.

2. Resolve the conflict by editing the file.

3. Once resolved, add the file and commit:

```
1  git add <conflicting_file>
2  git commit -m "Conflict resolution"
```

Description of Common Operations

Viewing Status

To see the current status of your repository and the changes made:

```
1  git status
```

Viewing the Commit History

You can get a record of all commits made with:

```
1  git log
```

Undoing Changes

If you make a change that you do not want to keep, you can undo uncommitted changes:

```
1  git checkout -- <file>
```

To undo a commit, you can use:

```
1  git reset --soft HEAD~1
```

This uncommits the last commit while keeping the changes in the staging area.

Integration with Remote Platforms

Git integrates seamlessly with collaboration platforms like GitHub, GitLab, and Bitbucket. These platforms allow you to collaborate on projects, manage branches, review changes, and perform pull requests.

Pushing Changes to a Remote Repository

To push your local repository to a remote one, first add the remote:

```
1   git remote add origin <remote_repository_url>
```

Then, to push your changes:

```
1   git push -u origin main
```

The -u flag sets an upstream reference, which makes future git push and git pull easier.

Pulling Changes from the Remote Repository

To synchronize your work with the changes made by others in the remote repository, you can use:

```
1   git pull origin main
```

Best Practices for Version Control

1. **Make Frequent Commits**: Making small, frequent commits makes it easier to identify problems and track changes.

2. **Write Descriptive Messages**: Make sure your commit messages are clear and describe the intention behind each change.

3. **Use Branches for New Features**: Work in separate branches for new features or fixes, allowing you to develop without affecting the

main branch.

4. **Keep Your Repository Clean**: Remove branches that are no longer needed after they've been merged.

5. **Document Significant Changes in a Changelog**: Keep track of significant changes in a changelog file to facilitate understanding of the project's evolution.

Conclusion

Version control with Git is a fundamental tool for any software developer. By mastering its features and workflows, you can improve collaboration, manage changes, and keep your project development on track. With proper use, Git not only allows you to have a clear history of your work but also helps you develop software more efficiently and organized. Take full advantage of this powerful tool, and you will see how it transforms your approach to developing and maintaining projects in artificial intelligence and beyond.